The Art of
Korean Cooking

The Art of
Korean Cooking

Onjium

Foreword by Woongchul Park
With over 120 illustrations

6	Foreword
10	Introduction: May Our Hope Become Our Wings
16	Korean Food, Flavours of Seonbi Imbued in Our Time

봄 Spring

20

66   Dishes of Onjium: Korean Food of Nature and Formality

여름 Summer
74

112   Essays on a Landscape: Gaeseong-bound

가을 Autumn
124

176   The Intricacy and Refinement of Goryeo Aesthetics

겨울 Winter
180

224	The Roots and Wings of Korean Food: Onjium's Goryeo Cuisine
232	The Gaeseong Food of Today
234	Onjium's Offering of Gaeseong Flavours
238	Onjium's Alcoholic Beverages
240	Onjium's Bugak
242	Onjium's Jangajji
246	Onjium's Tea
248	Onjium's Fruit and Vegetable Marmalades
250	About Onjium
250	Acknowledgments
251	About the Contributors
251	Photo Credits
252	Index

Foreword

Woongchul Park
*Founder / Chef,
Sollip Restaurant, London*

Korean cuisine is a living bridge between past and present. Rooted in nature, seasonality and time, it embodies the patience, thoughtfulness and quiet resilience that lie at the heart of Korean culture.

Working as a Korean chef in London, I have seen how Korean food has become more than just a cuisine; it has quietly emerged as a cultural language, resonating across the world. Korean food is not merely about flavours or techniques. It reflects a way of life where meals are shared and where thoughts and values are exchanged through the act of gathering. I believe the true strength of Korean cuisine lies in its ability to create community and forge connections between people.

Onjium's work captures this spirit with remarkable depth. Its efforts go beyond preserving the past; it breathes new life into recipes and ingredients shaped by centuries of tradition, weaving them naturally into the present. Onjium shows us that tradition is not something to be frozen in time but a living force – one that evolves and speaks anew to each generation.

In a world that moves ever faster, it is easy to lose touch with our roots and identity. Onjium reminds us that, when carried with care, the wisdom of the past can live meaningfully in the present and inspire the future. Its work is not about holding on to nostalgia, but about allowing heritage to grow – with dignity and purpose.

I hope this book offers readers a glimpse into the deep warmth, grace and communal spirit that define Korean food and culture.

Right:
Yuja (yuzu)

Page 2:
Gaeseong juak

Page 4:
Insam-jeonggwa

Page 8:
House-made *dasik* mould

Page 9:
Heukimja dasik

Introduction: May Our Hope Become Our Wings

Onjium – where we delve into the roots beneath our feet, unearth the wisdom and philosophy therein with the utmost care, and recount it by giving it inimitable voice.

Where we unwaveringly shore up and tend to the tastes of today so that the Korean food of the here and now, taken from the tides of tradition, may diffuse with ease through the everyday happenings of the present and continue to live on in the possibilities of tomorrow.

Our hope is that the warm and malleable flair and flavours of Onjium will constitute the beginning and the reverberations of understanding Korea and finding joy in what is ours.

Although the Joseon Dynasty ended relatively recently, Korea has faced turbulent times, including Japanese occupation, the Korean War and rapid economic development. In the pursuit of efficiency and productivity, many traditional values were neglected and phased out – values that are intrinsic to Korea's identity and cultural heritage. As modernization took precedence, much of this heritage was lost, and what remained was often poorly maintained, preserved only superficially, and left disconnected from contemporary life. A guardian of Korea's cultural foundation was urgently needed.

In response, the Arumjigi Culture Keepers Foundation was founded in 2001 as a steward of traditional culture. Over a decade later, in 2013, Onjium was established as a dedicated initiative to bring Arumjigi's vision to life, ensuring that Korea's rich cultural heritage is not only protected but also meaningfully integrated into modern society. This book serves as a record of Onjium's Food Studio, capturing its dedication to preserving and reinterpreting traditional Korean cuisine for future generations.

Onjium: Crafting Tomorrow's Heritage
Onjium is a creative lab where modern artisans shape the future by drawing on Korea's rich traditions of food, clothing and housing. With a vision to cultivate 'artisans of this time', Onjium fosters individuals who possess not only exceptional skill but also sound minds and refined sensibilities. These 'thinking hands' embody Onjium's philosophy, blending artistry with intellect to adapt heritage for contemporary society.

At Onjium, artisans are referred to as 'research fellows', emphasizing their roles as innovators and cultural custodians rather than mere practitioners. In the Food Studio, this distinction is particularly evident. Fellows delve into centuries-old noble family recipes, conduct field studies on regional cuisines, and explore disciplines such as ceramics, architecture and Oriental philosophy. This interdisciplinary approach enriches their understanding, enabling them to reinterpret traditional Korean cuisine with a modern aesthetic.

A Seasonal and Philosophical Approach to Food
Korea's compact yet geographically diverse land – home to mountains, fields and seas – has long provided an abundance of seasonal ingredients. Traditionally, Koreans embraced the agrarian rhythms of the land, creating dishes that celebrated nature's cycles. Fermented foods, which sustained communities through lean seasons, became central to the culinary identity, embodying both scientific ingenuity and philosophical depth.

At Onjium, this legacy is honoured by crafting seasonal, healthful dishes that reflect the natural rhythms of the land. Ingredients harvested at their peak are prepared with reverence, resulting in flavours that are both meaningful and delicious. The principle of 'simple but not shabby, brilliant but not extravagant' informs every aspect of Onjium's philosophy, from the balance of flavours to the design of table settings.

Journey to Authentic Flavours
Onjium travels to the sea and mountains in the pursuit of fresh ingredients and local flavours. Along the way, it often finds much more than expected. Onjium returns to Seoul carrying lessons learned from a countryside market stall, the rough fingertips of an aged mountain villager, the furrows on a distant island reached after half a day's boat ride, and the back of a fishing boat captain battling heavy seas with dreams of a full catch. Through these encounters, Onjium is reminded that what truly matters are the right season, the right time, our lives, and the strength of the foundation that sustains them.

'We can find fresh, precious ingredients harvested in a specific season only when we travel to the places where they are grown. But ingredients are not the only thing we seek. We meet people – the local experts who know best how to cultivate and prepare what their land offers. Little can be learned by staying in Seoul. This is the true meaning of Onjium's journey.' Research fellows at Onjium seek out ingredients unavailable in Seoul, ingredients that deserve wider recognition, and foods at risk of being forgotten. They learn the flavours of these local traditions and use them as the foundation for developing new recipes to share. Onjium embraces unfamiliar ingredients and bold approaches, drawing inspiration from these journeys. This inspiration, carefully refined, allows Onjium's dishes to continually evolve – dishes alive in the present, shaped by constant change and discovery.

Onjium's Twist
Everything changes over time, and culinary art is no exception. We cannot live with our traditions kept intact in our closets. What is important is that the 'culinary art of today' should be living 'today.' What kind of 'today' should we and our contemporaries create? This is a task and burden to be shared among ourselves and our contemporaries. Culinary art that moves towards tomorrow by embracing yesterday should imbue Korean food with originality while evading the trap of the tired old drive for 'modernization of tradition'.

'Korean cuisine has been handed down for thousands of years, and we have realized that endurance is required to cook Korean food. It is most important for us not to lose and forget its roots. Also important is to revive the values of Korean foods to suit this generation and hand them down to the next generation. The rich tastes unique to Korean food should be carried on. While developing foods of the nobility that suit the tastes of today, Onjium tries to make as few changes as possible. Only one or two ingredients are replaced with modern ingredients. If you focus on using good ingredients, the food tastes neither dated nor contrary to today's taste, even if the food is prepared according to old recipes. We at Onjium want to show how great old foods truly are without making many changes to them. Onjium seeks naturalness. We intend to preserve purity and perfect taste even without lavish recipes and diverse sauces, aiming at effectively presenting what we feel is

inherent to each food. To that end, the use of good ingredients is most important'.

The mindset and skill of the person preparing the dish are just as important. At Onjium, the true recipe lies in a discerning eye for the finest ingredients and in crafting each dish with care, love and heartfelt consideration.

It requires a dedication to preparing Korean food infused with a modern sense of beauty based on the foundation of tradition and prepared with healthy seasonal ingredients. This is the table of Korean foods prepared by Onjium. Ingredients from nature are marinated with tradition and then layers of tastes are added with love and affection. An everyday, ordinary meal table is made elegant and rich in flavour. May Onjium continue to present simple yet elegant Korean dishes through development and variation of taste that are quintessentially Onjium. May Onjium preserve the legacy of Korean food with affection and sincerity. And may this publication help Onjium venture forwards.

Joseon: The Roots of Elegance
Onjium's exploration of Korea's cultural traditions began with the Joseon dynasty, the period nearest to our own time and best documented in history. Over eight years, Onjium showcased the disciplined elegance of Joseon-era food, clothing and housing, with a particular focus on the traditions of noble families and the values upheld by virtuous scholars (seonbi).

'Tradition is spirit that maintains the shape, and it does not exist in its apparent shape', said Ando Tadao, the famous architect. Inspired by his idea of 'spirit that maintains the shape', Onjium took up the mission of reviving tradition to be true to our time. This partly involves making changes without losing the connection to the spirit of 'take the old to create the new'. Onjium's basic guideline is 검이불루 화이불치 (儉而不陋華而不侈), meaning 'making things simple but not shabby, brilliant but not extravagant'.

Joseon painting has both thick and light shades of ink, which are thick but not abundant and light but not faded. This is where the delicacy of Joseon painting lies.
Quote from 'Life is like a painting' by Son Cheol-ju

Onjium's creations embody dignified elegance through the wisdom of subtraction. Elegance that is neither rich nor poor. Each dish highlights the natural flavours of its ingredients, avoiding excessive garnishes and lavish presentations. This simplicity reflects the aesthetic values of the period, ensuring that every element serves a purpose.

Goryeo: A Golden Age of Culture and Cuisine
As Onjium's work evolved, it turned its attention to the Goryeo kingdom, a predecessor to Joseon renowned for its vibrant cultural exchanges and independent spirit. Goryeo's capital, Gaeseong, stood as a bustling centre of royalty and cosmopolitan culture for nearly 500 years, influencing the development of culinary and artistic traditions that continue to inspire.

Gaeseong cuisine epitomized the era's culinary sophistication, enriched by exchanges with neighbouring dynasties like Song, Yuan and Jin, as well as distant lands such as Japan and Arabia. Ingredients like sugar and black pepper arrived via the Song dynasty, while Yuan influence introduced meat-centric dishes featuring lamb. The period also saw the rise of raw fish dishes and a cosmopolitan flair in culinary presentation.

Beyond cuisine, Goryeo was a pinnacle of craftsmanship, producing jade-green celadon tea utensils, mother-of-pearl lacquerwork, metal crafts and Buddhist art. These creations, born of Goryeo's interactions with foreign cultures, reflect a refined elegance that continues to resonate today.

Left:
White gourd (*dongah*)

Preserving Korea's Culinary Legacy

Onjium stands as a guardian of tradition, dedicated to preserving its essence while seamlessly integrating it into modern life. By showcasing seasonal, wholesome dishes and refining traditional recipes with subtle contemporary touches, Onjium ensures that Korean cuisine remains rooted in its origins while resonating with contemporary diners. Each dish is a living testament to the enduring richness of Korea's culinary heritage.

Onjium's work is a tribute to Korea's history and an exploration of its future. By reconnecting with the deep strength of traditions from Joseon, Goryeo and beyond, Onjium bridges the past and present, enriching the lives and palates of today.

Onjium believes that the roots of Korean cuisine lie in food that embraces the seasons. Its intention is to take an active look at the distinctive plate that has naturally carved out a place for itself over this extended period. For a plate of food to arrive at its own form and take on its flavour, it must accumulate and weather the persistent changes brought about by the three elements – the lives of those who consume said cuisine, the environment in which it exists and the countless years intertwined between the two. The singular stories winnowed out of such history are condensed and told through plate upon plate of consummate taste.

This necessitates deliberating over the distinctive plate in order to share and experiment with our flavour-filled experiences. It has become more paramount than ever before to breathe life into the cultural vitality inherent to that plate and discover new horizons of possibility beyond it. In doing so, Onjium enables Korea's roots to spread their wings and travel greater distances in new form, thereby preserving what has been there throughout the ages before it slips from memory and existence.

Through its dedication to research, innovation and cultural preservation, Onjium fosters pride in Korea's heritage and inspires a sensitivity to the flavours, aesthetics and philosophies that define it. With each meal, Onjium offers a harmonious blend of rooted wisdom and modern artistry – a journey to uncover and celebrate the enduring beauty of Korean culture.

'The heart is the root dedicated to posterity. Without the planting of the root, there can be no flourishing of the branches and leaves.'
Hong Zicheng, Vegetable Roots Discourse (Caigentan)

Right:
Hairy crab (*teol-ge*)

All recipes in this book yield approximately four to five servings unless otherwise specified.

In Korean cuisine, it is common to season each ingredient separately before cooking, in a process called *mitgan* ('pre-seasoning'). Because the main ingredients and the flavour of fermented sauces used are unique to individual households, the quantities of the seasonings used in this step are hard to standardize. Therefore, in many recipes ingredients for *mitgan* seasonings – salt, pepper, flour, starch powder, oil, onion, crushed garlic etc – are intentionally not given a fixed amount. This flexibility is a defining characteristic of Korean cuisine, but in most cases a small measure (pinch, dash, teaspoon or tablespoon) is appropriate.

Korean Food, Flavours of Seonbi Imbued in Our Time

Yun Gyun S. Hong
*Chair of Board of Directors,
Onjium*

Over the years, Korean culture has transcended borders, captivating the world with its vibrant pop culture at the forefront. What began as an interest in music, film and television has blossomed into a deeper exploration of Korea's rich heritage, including its cuisine. Today, interest in Korean culture has reached unprecedented heights both at home and abroad, with Korean food emerging as a vital aspect of global cultural and artistic discourse, inviting audiences around the world to engage with its flavours, traditions and aesthetics, in turn sparking a growing curiosity about the true essence of Korean cuisine and a deeper appreciation for its rich culinary heritage.

This publication is a quest to rediscover and revive Korean cuisine, adapting it to suit the contemporary palate while preserving its inherent spirit, taste and beauty in dishes for today. Onjium has drawn inspiration from the cuisine of the Joseon dynasty's nobility, which was influenced by royal traditions, to identify meals that promote health and wellbeing for modern lifestyles. The noble cuisine of the Joseon era was defined by its simplicity, balanced nutrition and understated beauty. It was neither salty nor spicy, and celebrated the tastes and flavours inherent to the ingredients. It offers an excellent timeless model of healthy food and dietary habits for modern people. However, Onjium's goal is not merely to replicate the cuisine of the Joseon nobility and royal family. Instead, Onjium seeks to adapt and modernize them, incorporating elements from recipes discovered in old Joseon cookbooks, traditional Western recipes, contemporary culinary practices and recipes commonly used today, and even local cuisine and familiar street foods. These influences are thoughtfully integrated to create 'modernized ordinary dishes of the Joseon nobility', preserving the essence and natural flavours inherent to each ingredient while making the cuisine relevant and appealing to today's palate.

Culture evolves through the ages, yet its core archetypes remain enduring. Korean culture is still alive and thriving in everyday life, shaped by its rich history and the spirit of each era. Korean culture has always been informed by the zeitgeist; the spirit of the times. At its heart lies the *seonbi spirit* – a philosophy that values spiritual fulfilment over material gain, prioritizes consideration for others before one's own interest, embraces modernity and exercises caution against excess. This ethos aligns with traditional Korean aesthetics, encapsulated by the saying, 'Make it simple without being shabby, and (make) it brilliant without being extravagant.' It also shares the same values as the teachings of Confucius, who said in the Confucian Analects, 'When there is the right balance of raw material and refinement, you get a gentleman.' He continued, 'Where the solid qualities are in excess of accomplishments, we have rusticity; where the accomplishments are in excess of the solid qualities, we have the manners of a clerk. When the accomplishments and solid qualities are equally blended, we then have the man of virtue.' The refined beauty cherished by Korean tradition has accordingly blossomed naturally from the harmony between content and form, grounded in the spirit of moderation and the middle way. This same principle applies to the beauty found in traditional Korean cuisine, where simplicity and elegance coexist. The presentation and preparation of each dish embody harmony, combining classical simplicity with refined sophistication. This balance of raw material and refined craftsmanship defines Korean food – and achieving this harmony is the central objective of Onjium.

Many types of Korean food have been studied, including royal court food, temple food and seasonal dishes. However, the spirit behind the food and the beauty that reflects that spirit has seldom been examined. Onjium's aim is to revive the taste, spirit and aesthetics of traditional Korean cuisine by crafting dishes that blend timeless values with contemporary sensibilities. By modernizing everyday meals of the Joseon nobility, Onjium strives to make them relevant and appealing to today's society. These dishes are carefully prepared – neat, healthy and well presented – making them ideal for special occasions or honoured guests. Despite their simplicity, they are served with genuine hospitality and courtesy, reflecting a culinary culture rich in both taste and spirit. A table set with no rigid rules on the number of dishes embodies a philosophy of mindfulness and humility – values rooted in a deep respect for the environment and for others. This time-honoured spirit of Korean culture, where meals nourish both body and soul, represents a uniquely Korean approach to dining. It is this profound connection to tradition that Onjium seeks to rediscover and share with the world today.

There is a saying: 'Technology is to be imitated, but culture is to be longed for.' In an age of material abundance, the pursuit of spiritual value has become a new driving force for cultural evolution. If the timeless seonbi spirit aligns with the zeitgeist of the 21st century, it can foster a vibrant and thriving culture for our times. Onjium's mission is to present authentic Korean cuisine rooted in the essence of tradition. Its dedicated research fellows can be seen as the 'new artisans of the 21st century', shaping the spirit of the age while drawing from the enduring foundation of cultural archetypes.

Every day, Koreans connect with the spirit and essence of their culture through the simplicity and care of a neatly set table. It is my hope that the beauty of modesty and consideration for others represented by the daily setting of a table will merge with the joyful and creative dynamics of Korean culture, evolving into a richer Korean culinary tradition to be shared with the world. This simple yet elegant way of life, rooted in spiritual values, is the quintessence of Korean culture – an offering of timeless significance in this age of globalization.

Previous page:
Bamboo shoot (*juksun*)

Right:
Shingled hedgehog mushroom (*neungi-beoseot*)

봄

SPRING

will surely come as always

SPRING

방풍죽
Bangpung-juk
Rice porridge with bangpung leaves

Koreans have long cherished the herb known as *bangpung* (wild parsnip leaves). Heo Gyun, a literati and bureaucrat of the Joseon dynasty, mentioned it in 1611 during his exile in his book on food, *Domundaejak*. *Bangpung* is a coastal herb that thrives in sea winds and is known for its effectiveness in preventing strokes. The *bangpung* from Geumodo Island in Yeosu, on the south coast, is especially prized.

Ingredients
120 g (⅔ cup) rice
10 cm (4 in.) square piece of dried kelp (*dasima*)
20 g (¾ oz) dried anchovy (*myeolchi*), heads and innards removed
10 g (⅓ oz) large-eyed herring fish (*dipori*)
1 L (4¼ cups) water
70 g (2½ oz) *bangpung* (wild parsnip leaves)
1 tbsp pine nuts, coarsely ground
salt

Dasima myeolchi stock
1 sheet of dried kelp
70 g (2½ oz) dried anchovy, heads and innards removed
2 L (2 qts ½ cup) water
Korean soy sauce (*guk-ganjang*)
salt

Making the stock
Stir the dried anchovy (*myeolchi*) and large-eyed herring fish (*dipori*) in a dry frying pan for 1 minute at a low heat. Boil 2 L (2 qts ½ cup) of cold water with a sheet of dried kelp (*dasima*). Remove the dried kelp when the water begins to boil. Turn the heat to low and simmer for 40 minutes. Strain through a sieve lined with muslin.

Method
- Wash the rice in several changes of water and soak in water for 2 hours. Strain in a colander and grind coarsely.
- Pick tender *bangpung* (wild parsnip leaves), wash under running water, and strain well.
- Boil the ground rice in *dasima myeolchi* stock (recipe below left) over a high heat. Simmer for about 15 minutes until the water is completely absorbed. Add the *bangpung* and simmer for 5 minutes.
- Remove from the heat. Sprinkle with ground pine nuts. Season with salt.

SPRING

석류만두
Seokryu-mandu
Pomegranate dumpling

Shaped like a pomegranate, hence the name, this dumpling was served in the royal household and was traditionally stuffed with vegetables such as sweet white radish, *minari* (Korean watercress) and boneless chicken. Onjium has created a variety of this royal dumpling, adding a modern twist. We've changed the colour and texture of the wrappers by incorporating spring mugwort into the dough and rolling out the discs thinly. The pomegranate dumpling makes for a stunning presentation, whether steamed or boiled in soup.

Dumpling filling
1 courgette (zucchini), seeded and shredded
100 g (3½ oz) white radish, shredded
50 g (1¾ oz) beef, finely minced
40 g (1½ oz) shingled hedgehog mushroom (*neungi-beoseot*)*, shredded
50 g (1¾ oz) onion, finely minced
50 g (1¾ oz) tofu
30 g (1 oz) *minari* (Korean watercress)
400 ml (1⅔ cups) beef brisket broth
salt

Dough for dumpling wrappers
150 g (1½ cups) flour
½ tbsp egg white
½ tbsp grape seed oil
salt
mugwort powder
25 ml (¹⁄₁₀ cup) water

Seasoning for courgette (zucchini)
chopped spring onion (scallion)
crushed garlic
roasted sesame seeds
sesame oil

Seasoning for white radish
chopped spring onion
crushed garlic
ginger juice

Method
- To make the dumpling filling, julienne the courgette (zucchini) into strips 3 cm (1¼ in.) long (discard seeds). Sprinkle with salt. Let stand for 10 minutes. Squeeze excess water from courgette, and stir-fry in a pan. Add seasoning for courgette. Soak white radish in lightly salted water for 10 minutes. Strain and squeeze out excess water. Stir-fry in a pan. Add seasoning. Stir-fry the beef and mushroom. Stir-fry the onion. Remove excess water from tofu and mash. Blanch the *minari* (Korean watercress) in boiling water. Strain and chop. Mix all the ingredients prepared above in a large bowl. Season with salt.
- To make the dumpling wrapper dough, whisk all the ingredients in a large bowl. For the best results, let the dough rest for several hours to mature. Roll out the dough into thin circles, one for each dumpling.
- Place a portion of filling in the centre of each wrapper. Pull up the edges of the dough around the filling to form a cylinder, leaving the top open so that the filling is visible, resembling a pomegranate.
- Place the dumplings in a steamer basket set over boiling water and steam for 5 minutes. Meanwhile, season the brisket broth with salt and bring to a boil. Arrange the dumplings on a plate and drizzle with the hot broth just before serving.

* The shingled hedgehog mushroom is an aromatic, wild mushroom used in Korean cooking.

SPRING

대하전복육즙무침
Daeha jeonbok yukjeup-muchim
Prawn and abalone with beef gravy

This is a light, refreshing cold dish for spring. Large prawns (shrimp), abalones and spring vegetables are mixed in beef gravy. To prepare the delicious beef broth, the beef is sautéed first and then water is added to it. Lightly seasoned, the unique flavour of each ingredient can be appreciated. When the beef broth is prepared in advance and kept cool for a couple of hours, it becomes thicker, which makes mixing much easier. Mix ingredients immediately before serving to prevent the vegetables from becoming mushy.

Ingredients
2 abalones, scrubbed and innards removed
½ spring onion (scallion), cut in 5 cm (2 in.) long slices
4 jumbo prawns (shrimp), heads removed (but keep)
100 g (3½ oz) bamboo shoots (*juksun*)
⅓ Korean pear, peeled
4 asparagus spears, peeled
100 g (3½ oz) minced beef
cheongju (Korean rice wine)

To boil prawns (shrimp)
spring onion
lemon
onion
salt

Seasoning for beef
soy sauce
sugar
chopped spring onion
crushed garlic
sesame oil
pepper

Seasoning for beef gravy
vinegar
honey
salt
mustard

Method
- Place the abalones shell-side down in a basket set over boiling water. Drizzle *cheongju* (Korean rice wine) over the abalones. Top with the spring onion (scallion) and steam for 1½ hours. Remove the abalone meat from the shells. Slice the meat.
- Skewer the prawns (shrimp). Boil the skewered prawns, the heads and ingredients for boiling prawns together for 2 minutes.
- Cool the prawns and cut in half diagonally.
- Peel off the outer skin of the bamboo shoots (*juksun*) and boil in water for 1 hour. Let cool in cold water to remove bitterness. Cut the boiled bamboo shoots in half, then slice to reveal their comb-like pattern.
- Cut the pear into 6 portions. Cut each portion diagonally into thick slices.
- Blanch the asparagus in boiling water. Cut into pieces 4cm (1½ in.) long.
- Season the minced beef and stir-fry, adding water little by little to make beef gravy. Let it cool. Season with vinegar, honey, salt and mustard.
- Mix all ingredients in beef gravy and arrange on a plate.

SPRING

육면젓국구이
Yuk-myeon jeontguk-gui
Grilled beef noodle seasoned with pickled prawn sauce

This dish is inspired by a recipe from *Suunjapbang*, a cookbook dating from the early Joseon period, which states: 'Half cook rich meat, cut thinly like noodles and add to soup.' The interesting texture of the long, noodle-like pieces of beef, along with the use of *saeujeot* (fermented prawn/shrimp) instead of soy sauce for seasoning, gives this dish its distinctive character.

Ingredients
600 g (1 lb 5⅛ oz) beef sirloin
160 ml (⅔ cup) Korean pear juice
2 eggs (to make ribbons for garnish)
ground pine nuts

Steak marinade
1 tbsp *saeujeot* (fermented prawn/shrimp)
1 tsp Korean soy sauce (*guk-ganjang*)
salt
1 tbsp honey
3 tbsps cooking wine
3 tbsps pear juice
2 tbsps chopped spring onion (scallion)
1 tbsp crushed garlic
2 tbsps sesame oil
1 tbsp roasted sesame seeds

Method
- Cut the steak into long, thick, angular strips. Soak in the pear juice for 1 hour to remove blood. Marinate in steak marinade for 1 hour.
- Barbecue or pan fry the steak.
- Beat the egg whites and yolks separately and make thin white omelettes and yellow omelettes. Cut into ribbon-like strips.
- Place the steak on a plate, top with the egg ribbons and sprinkle with the ground pine nuts.

SPRING

움파불고기
Wumpa bulgogi
Bulgogi with spring onion

The yellowish heart of the spring onion (scallion) stalk, which endures the cold winter and is harvested in the spring, is especially tender and savoury. Onjium presents the grilled *bulgogi* – which literally translates to 'fire meat' – made tender by mixing chicken, sirloin and bamboo shoots (*juksun*), along with seasoned spring onions, for a refreshing spring meal.

Ingredients
300 g (10½ oz) sirloin, finely shredded
200 g (7 oz) chicken meat, minced
20 g (¾ oz) fruits from *maesil-cheong* (plum marmalade), seeded and finely minced
50 g (1¾ oz) Korean pear, finely minced
30 g (1 oz) onion, finely minced
2 spring onions (scallions), cut into 5 cm (2 in.) long strips
ground pine nuts

Bulgogi sauce
1½ tbsp soy sauce
1 tsp Korean soy sauce (*guk-ganjang*)
1 tbsp honey
1 tsp sugar
1 tbsp chopped spring onion
1 tsp crushed garlic
1 tbsp sesame oil
pepper

Method
- Mix the sirloin, chicken meat, plum fruits, pear and onion with *bulgogi* sauce and knead.
- Stir-fry the spring onion (scallion) in a frying pan until slightly cooked.
- If using a barbecue, once the charcoal is lit, place the grill rack with the meat on top and cook together with the spring onion. Alternatively, you can use a frying pan.
- Place the meat on a warm plate. Top with the spring onion. Sprinkle with the ground pine nuts.

오곡밥과 아홉나물
Ogokbap and ahop namul
Five-grain rice and eight vegetables

On the Great Full Moon of the First Month, which falls on the 15th day of the first lunar month, Koreans enjoy a dish called *ogokbap*, a rice made from five kinds of grain, hard-shelled nuts, *yaksik* (sweetened rice with dried fruits and nuts), and other seasonal foods. Traditionally, they would share a bowl of *ogokbap* and carefully prepared dried vegetable dishes with their neighbours, praying for health and peace in the new year.

Five-grain rice

360 g (2 cups) glutinous rice, washed, soaked in water for 4 hours and strained
90 g (½ cup) red beans, washed and strained
90 g (½ cup) black beans, washed, soaked in water for 3 hours and strained
90 g (½ cup) glutinous African millet, washed, soaked in water for 3 hours and strained
60 g (⅓ cup) glutinous millet, washed, soaked in water for 3 hours and strained

Method
- Put the red beans and scalding water into a pan, and heat for 2 minutes at a high heat. When it boils, discard the water. Add fresh water to the sweet red beans, and heat it up for 3 minutes on a high heat. Lower the heat to medium, boil for 20 minutes, taking care to prevent the beans from bursting, and then strain. Set aside the water used to boil the red beans to cook the rice in later.
- Spread muslin on a basket over boiling water in the steamer. Mix the glutinous rice, black beans, glutinous African millet and glutinous millet and place in the steamer. Steam for 40 minutes in total. After about 20 minutes, gently sprinkle the red-bean liquid, seasoned with salt, over the rice. Also add the red beans. Continue steaming for the remaining 20 minutes. The steaming time may vary depending on the amount of rice.
- When the rice is cooked, turn off the heat and let it sit for 10 minutes.

Eight vegetables

70 g (2½ oz) dried *gosari* (bracken), soaked in water for 1 hour
50 g (1¾ oz) dried sliced squash, soaked in water for 1 hour
300 g (10½ oz) fresh white radish, cut into 5cm (2 in.) long thin strips
200 g (7 oz) fresh spinach
70 g (2½ oz) dried *sannamul* (wild greens), soaked in water for 1 hour, boiled until tender and rinsed with cold water
70 g (2½ oz) dried *chwinamul* (aster), soaked in water for 1 hour, boiled until tender and rinsed with cold water
200 g (7 oz) fresh *doraji* (bellflower root), peeled and cut into thin strips
50 g (1¾ oz) dried aubergine (eggplant), soaked in water for 1 hour and cut into 5 cm (2 in.) long pieces

Seasoning for vegetables

Korean soy sauce (*guk-ganjang*)
salt
chopped spring onion (scallion)
crushed garlic
roasted sesame seeds
perilla seed oil
ginger juice

Recipe continues on next page

Method

- Blanch the *gosari* (bracken) in boiling water until soft (about 30 minutes). Rinse thoroughly with cold water and cut into pieces 5 cm (2 in.) in length. Season the *gosari* with Korean soy sauce (*guk-ganjang*), chopped spring onion (scallion), crushed garlic and perilla seed oil. Stir-fry the *gosari* for 3–4 minutes. Add 1 tablespoon of water and stir-fry for 5 minutes on a low heat. Sprinkle with roasted sesame seeds.
- Cut the slices of squash in half and season with salt, chopped spring onion, crushed garlic and sesame oil, then stir-fry.
- Add a pinch of salt to the white radish and set aside for 20 minutes. Squeeze out any excess water from the white radish strips. Stir-fry the white radish in an oiled pan. Add 1 tablespoon of water, chopped spring onion, crushed garlic, ginger juice and perilla seed oil, then stir-fry.
- Blanch the spinach in boiling water (add a pinch of salt). Rinse with cold water. Squeeze out any excess water from the spinach. Season with chopped spring onion, crushed garlic, sesame oil and ground sesame seeds.
- Season the *sannamul* (wild greens) and *chwinamul* (aster) with Korean soy sauce, chopped spring onion, crushed garlic and sesame oil, and stir-fry in an oiled pan. Add 2 tablespoons of water and stir-fry until softened over a low heat.
- Add salt to the *doraji* (bellflower root) and rub to remove the bitterness. Stir-fry in an oiled pan. Add chopped spring onion and crushed garlic and continue to stir-fry until tender.
- Stir-fry the aubergine (eggplant) in an oiled pan. Add chopped spring onion and crushed garlic, Korean soy sauce and salt, and stir-fry for another 3 minutes. Add perilla seed oil and sprinkle with roasted sesame seeds.

SPRING

봄나물 비빔밥
Bomnamul bibimbap
Bibimbap with spring vegetables

Koreans have long enjoyed *bibimbap*, rice mixed with various ingredients to create a unique flavour. Onjium's version of *bibimbap* differs from typical *bibimbap*, which is topped with colourful ingredients, by featuring only vegetables harvested in spring. Serve with seasoned sauce made of *eundallae jangajji* (pickled wild onion) to enhance the taste of the rice.

Ingredients
360 g (2 cups) rice
540 ml (2¼ cups) water
50 g (1¾ oz) *chwinamul* (aster)
50 g (1¾ oz) *wonchuri* (daylilies)
50 g (1¾ oz) *bangpung* (wild parsnip leaves)
60 g (2 oz) *dureup* (fatsia shoot)
60 g (2 oz) *naengi* (shepherd's purse)

Seasoning for vegetables
Korean soy sauce (*guk-ganjang*)
salt
chopped spring onion (scallion)
minced garlic
sesame oil

Seasoning for soy sauce
eundallae jangajji (pickled wild onion)
chives
green pepper
red pepper
roasted sesame seeds
sesame oil

Method
- Wash the rice. Soak in water for 30 minutes.
- Remove the tough parts of the stems of the *chwinamul* (aster) and clean it. Parboil the *chwinamul* in boiling water with a dash of salt.
- Cook the rice in a pot. Add the parboiled *chwinamul*, to the pot when the water has almost evaporated.
- Clean the *wonchuri* (daylilies), *bangpung* (wild parsnip leaves), *dureup* (fatsia shoot) and *naengi* (shepherd's purse), and parboil in boiling water with a dash of salt. Plunge in ice water, then squeeze with your hands to remove any excess water. Mix with vegetable seasoning.
- Mix the cooked rice with *chwinamul* evenly. Scoop the rice into a bowl and put the seasoned vegetables on top. Serve with soy sauce seasoning.

봄나물 비빔밥
Bomnamul bibimbap

SPRING

도미찜
Domi-jjim
Stuffed and steamed red snapper

Called *domi* in Korean, red snapper tastes best in spring. Once considered a delicacy, it is still cherished today for its deliciously light and soft flavour. Steamed red snapper, stuffed with various ingredients and tied with straw, has been passed down through generations by the Heo family clan in Jisu-myeon, Gyeongsangnam-do Province. Onjium prepares *domi-jjim* with the bones removed.

Ingredients
1 red snapper
250 g (8¾ oz) mung bean sprouts, heads and tails removed
170 g (6 oz) *minari* (Korean watercress),
    cut into 3 cm (1¼ in.) long pieces
2–3 fresh shiitake mushrooms, shredded
80 g (2¾ oz) beef, shredded
flour
salt
pepper

Seasoning for beef
soy sauce
sugar
chopped spring onion (scallion)
minced garlic
roasted sesame seeds
sesame oil
pepper

Seasoning for fish filling
Korean soy sauce (*guk-ganjang*)
salt
chopped spring onion
minced garlic
sesame oil
1 egg

Method
- Scale the red snapper. Cut the fish open and remove the bones.
- Soak the fish in lightly salted water for 30 minutes. Pat dry to remove any excess moisture from the fish.
- Season the shiitake with salt and pepper. Stir-fry. Mix the beef with seasoning. Stir-fry to medium rare. Mix the *minari* (Korean watercress), mung bean sprouts, shiitake and beef with the seasoning for the fish filling to make the stuffing.
- Sprinkle the inside of the fish with flour and fill with the stuffing. Tie the fish closed with straw.
- Put 480–720 ml (2–3 cups) of water in a large pan, and place a steamer tray inside. Bring the water to the boil. Steam the fish on the steamer tray for about 20 minutes, then let it stand for 5 minutes. Steaming time varies depending on the size of the fish.
- Remove the fish from the steamer and cut into bite-sized pieces. Arrange the vegetables and the fish on a large plate.

SPRING

해물전골
Haemul jeongol
Seafood hot pot

Hot pot, called *jeongol* in Korean, refers to elaborate Korean stews or casseroles made with a main ingredient and various minor ingredients, all boiled together in broth. At Onjium, small pancakes of cod fillet, prawn (shrimp), *minari* (Korean watercress), mushrooms and octopus are added to the *jeongol*, enhancing the dish with a rich and refreshing flavour.

Ingredients
½ cod
3 abalones
½ spring onion (scallion), cut in pieces 3 cm (1¼ in.) long
150 g (5¼ oz) mid-sized prawns (shrimp),
    skinned and chopped
2 small octopuses
70 g (2½ oz) *minari* (Korean watercress),
    cut in pieces 3 cm (1¼ in.) long
50 g (1¾ oz) *euni* mushrooms
10 g (⅓ oz) *seogi* mushrooms*
4 eggs
7 walnuts
10 ginkgo nuts
60 g (½ cup) flour
cheongju (Korean rice wine)

Seasoning for prawn (shrimp) pancake
chopped spring onion
minced garlic
ginger juice
sesame oil

Cod stock
300 g (10½ oz) white radish
10 cm (4 in.) square dried kelp (*dasima*)
30 g (1 oz) ginger
2 L (2 qts ½ cup) water

Method
- Remove the innards and bones from the cod. Rinse and slice the cod into 8–9 pieces 4 cm (1½ in.) long at a 45-degree angle. Sprinkle a few pinches of salt over the slices. Set the head and bones aside.
- Beat all 4 eggs in a small bowl; the mixture will be used for all the pancakes. Dip each slice of cod in the beaten eggs, and place it on a heated pan and cook both sides.
- Put the cod head and bones and ingredients for cod stock into a pot of cold water. Remove the kelp (*dasima*) when the water starts boiling. Boil for about 1 hour at a low heat. After the first 30 minutes of boiling, the white radish should be well done. Remove the white radish and slice into squares. Sieve the cod stock through cotton gauze. Season with salt.
- Place the abalones shell-side down in a basket set over boiling water. Drizzle *cheongju* (Korean rice wine) over them. Top with the spring onion (scallion) and steam for 1½ hours. Remove the abalone meat from the shells and cut into 3 or 4 pieces.
- Mix the prawns (shrimp) with 1 tbsp flour, pancake seasoning and 2 tbsps of the beaten-egg mixture. Spoon portions into a lightly oiled pan, flatten and pan-fry.
- Turn the head of the small octopus inside out. Gently but firmly remove the innards and the ink sac, and discard, taking care not to break the ink sac. Rinse under clean running water. Put into boiling water. Remove immediately and put into ice water to cool it down. Wipe with cotton cloth and slice into pieces 5 cm long.
- Cut the *minari* (Korean watercress) into 3 cm (1¼ in.) long pieces. Combine the *minari* with 2 tbsps flour and 160 ml (⅔ cup) of the beaten-egg, mixing well. Spoon the mixture onto a lightly oiled pan and pan-fry until golden. Blanch a few strands of *minari* (to be used for tying the octopus).
- Tie the sliced octopus with the blanched *minari* strands.
- Soak the *euni* mushrooms in water for about 30 minutes. Cut into bite-size pieces.
- Soak the *seogi* mushrooms in water for about 30 minutes. Finely mince and mix with egg white. Pan-fry and cut into thin strips. Peel the walnuts and ginkgo nuts.
- Arrange all the prepared ingredients in a large round pot. Garnish with walnuts and ginkgo nuts. Pour in the seasoned cod stock and bring to the boil.

* *Seogi* mushrooms are wild edible mushrooms, often dried and used in Korean cooking.

SPRING

진달래 화전
Jindallae hwajeon
Azalea rice cake

Garnished with edible azalea flowers, known as *jindallae* in Korean, which grow wild in the mountains during spring, this seasonal rice cake captures the essence of the season. In the past, Koreans would venture into the mountains in early spring to enjoy nature and pick azaleas, placing the flowers on top of pan-fried rice cake. While honey is commonly used as a sweetener, Onjium uses yuja (yuzu) citron marmalade to bring out the spring flavour instead.

Ingredients
200 g (2 cups) glutinous rice flour
5 tbsps of boiling water
azalea blossoms
yuja (yuzu) citron marmalade

Method
- Add hot water to the rice flour and mix well to create a dough. Knead the dough until soft, then divide it into 20 equal-sized pieces. Roll each piece into a ball with your hands. Press each ball into a disc about 4 cm (1½ in.) in diameter.
- Heat up a pan over a medium-high heat. Add vegetable oil to coat the surface. Put the rice cakes in the pan and cook them for a few minutes. When the bottoms are slightly crispy, turn them over and flatten them out. Cook for a few more minutes.
- Place the rice cakes on a plate and top with azaleas just before serving. Finally, drizzle the yuja (yuzu) citron marmalade over them.

SPRING

탕평채
Tangpyeong-chae
Mung bean jelly salad with vegetables and beef

Nokdu, or mung beans, have been cultivated in Korea since before 57 BC, during the Three Kingdoms Period. A versatile and easy-to-handle ingredient, *nokdu* has long been a favourite in Korean cuisine. *Cheongpo-muk*, a hardened mung bean starch that looks very much like white jelly, is often tossed with various vegetables to make *tangpyeong-chae*. Onjium's version reimagines this dish as it might have been during the Goryeo dynasty, before carrots were introduced to the peninsula. It presents a well-balanced combination of flavours and colours.

Ingredients
1 pack or 300 g (10½ oz) *cheongpo-muk* (mung bean jelly)
70 g (2½ oz) lean beef
100 g (3½ oz) poached shiitake mushrooms
2 abalones
1 dried sea cucumber, soaked in water
½ *aehobak* (a type of Korean summer squash)
1 Korean cucumber
70 g (2½ oz) *deodeok* (lance asiabell roots)
150 g (5¼ oz) mung bean sprouts
2 medium-sized eggs
½ bunch spring onion (scallion), sliced once lengthwise
drizzle of sake
salt
minced spring onion
crushed garlic
pine nut powder

Beef marinade
½ tsp salt
1 tsp sugar
½ tbsp minced spring onion
1 tsp crushed garlic
1 tsp sesame oil
black pepper

Poached shiitake mushrooms
500 g (1 lb 1⅝ oz) dried shiitake mushrooms soaked in water
6 tbsps soy sauce
6 tbsps sugar
2 tbsps cooking oil
5 tbsps vinegar
1 tbsp sesame oil
1½ tbsps oligosaccharide syrup

Recipe continues on next page

Method

- Soak the dried shiitake mushrooms in water, slice thinly and cut into julienne strips.
- Bring soy sauce and sugar to the boil, then add the mushroom strips and a little water.
- Once the moisture disappears, add vinegar, sesame oil and oligosaccharide syrup. Continue to stir-fry until the sauce soaks in.
- Slice the refrigerated *cheongpo-muk* (mung bean jelly) thinly into julienne strips.
- Cut the beef into 4 cm (1½ in.) long pieces, freeze it slightly to cut into julienne strips, and massage the marinade in, then pan-fry.
- Prepare the poached shiitake mushrooms (see recipe on page 44).
- Wash the abalones thoroughly and place them on a steamer. Sprinkle with sake, cover with the sliced spring onions (scallions), and steam for about 1½ hours. Allow to chill, then slice thinly into julienne strips.
- Drain the water-soaked sea cucumber, season it with soy sauce and sesame oil, sauté it in a pan, and then cut it into thin strips.
- Chop the *aehobak* (Korean summer squash) into 5 cm (2 in.) long pieces, peel each entire piece into one long sheet (*dolryeokkaki*) and julienne.
- Sprinkle salt, then let it sit. Heat the pan, coat it with oil and pan-fry.
- Prepare the cucumber the same way as the *aehobak*, but chop it in a longer length of 5 cm (2 in.). Peel each block into one long sheet, julienne, sprinkle with salt and let it sit for a while. Pan-fry.
- Peel the *deodeok* (lance asiabell roots) and slice first at an angle, then julienne. Sauté with the chopped spring onion and crushed garlic in an oil-coated pan.
- Trim off the heads and tails of the mung bean sprouts, and blanch them in boiling, salted water.
- Separate the egg whites and yolks, then make two omelettes (one white and one yellow). Cut each one into julienne strips. Note: This is a popular topping in Korean cuisine, known as *jidan*.
- Blanch the mung bean jelly strips in boiling water, drain well and season with salt and sesame oil.
- Place the mung bean jelly strips in the centre of a serving dish and carefully surround the jelly strips with each group of ingredients. Toss well at the dinner table and sprinkle with the pine nut powder before eating.

Notes

- Season each ingredient lightly as the taste will become stronger once they are added together.
- Be sure to blanch the *cheongpo-muk* at the very end. Otherwise, the jelly strips may stick and become one big lump by the time you try to toss the ingredients.
- The poached shiitake mushroom strips are useful for other Korean dishes too. Feel free to make plenty.
- Many *tangpyeong-chae* recipes you see out in the world will not include abalones. Trust us and try adding steamed, julienned abalones. It will be a pleasant surprise.

SPRING

복탕
Bok-tang
Pufferfish soup

Since ancient times, pufferfish has been considered a precious delicacy, earning the nickname *hadon*, meaning 'a piglet caught in the river'. Records of pufferfish consumption date back as early as the Goryeo period. Pufferfish are caught in the lower reaches of the Hangang and Imjingang Rivers around the time when peach flowers bloom, as they migrate upstream to spawn. Those caught at this time are prized for their exceptional flavour. To prepare *bok-tang*, pufferfish fillets are lightly coated with starch powder for a smooth texture, and sesame water is added to the broth for a rich, distinctive taste. It is one springtime delicacy you do not want to miss.

Note
Pufferfish is poisonous, so always handle with extreme care.

Ingredients
1 kg (2 lb 4 oz) river pufferfish (*hwang-bok*)
1 L (4¼ cups) water
dried kelp (*dasima*)
200 g (7 oz) bamboo shoots (*juksun*)
1 Korean cucumber
½ pack tofu
100 g (3½ oz) napa cabbage
1 farm-grown pine mushroom (*cham-songyi-beoseot*)
1 cup hulled sesame seeds
starch powder
salt

Method
- Clean, skin and bone the river pufferfish (*hwang-bok*) and remove blood by rinsing the head and bones in running water.
- Make a clear broth by boiling the dried kelp (*dasima*) and river pufferfish together. Remove the river pufferfish and slice the meat thinly. Set aside the broth for later.
- Cook the bamboo shoots (*juksun*) and slice thinly at an angle. Cut the cucumber lengthwise to remove the seeds, then slice it into thin rectangular pieces (known as *golpae* shape in Korean culinary arts), approximately 3 cm (1¼ in.) by 2 cm (¾ in.).
- Prepare the tofu, napa cabbage and farm-grown pine mushroom (*cham-songyi-beoseot*) into a similar shape or length.
- Transfer 1.7 L (7 cups) of river pufferfish broth and hulled sesame seeds to a blender, grind them finely, then strain the liquid through a muslin to filter out the remaining sediment.
- Heat the sesame soup, and as it begins to boil, add the river pufferfish meat, vegetables and tofu lightly coated with starch powder. Season with salt and turn off the heat after it returns to a boil.

SPRING

전복꽃찜
Jeonbok-kkot-jjim
Steamed abalone with root vegetables

Abalones have long been considered a delicacy. For this dish, the abalones are scored, filled with fish and tofu, and then steamed. Onjium's version is topped with julienned and seasoned autumn *deodeok* (lance asiabell roots) and *doraji* (bellflower roots). With the white interiors of the roots arranged over the steamed abalones, the dish resembles blooming flowers – hence the name *kkot-jjim* (literally, 'flower-steamed dish').

Ingredients
5 fresh abalones
drizzle of sake
1 bunch of spring onions (scallions)
240 ml (1 cup) beef broth
Korean soy sauce (*guk-ganjang*)
salt

Stuffing
70 g (2½ oz) prawn (shrimp)
50 g (1¾ oz) tofu
a little chopped spring onion
a little crushed garlic
sesame oil
salt

Namul, or seasoned Korean herbs
2 fresh *doraji* (bellflower roots)
2 fresh *deodeok* (lance asiabell roots)
⅙ Korean radish
2 shiitake mushrooms
3 Korean chestnuts
minced spring onion

Method
- Clean and prepare the abalones. Put the abalones in a heated steamer, drizzle over sake, cover with spring onion (scallion) and cook for about 1½ hours. Score the abalones at an angle, 4–5 times.

Making the stuffing
- Mince the prawns (shrimp) and mash the tofu. Chop the onion, sprinkle with salt, then drain the water to pan-fry.
- Mix the prawns, tofu and onions together, and season with minced spring onion, crushed garlic and sesame oil. Fill the scored abalones with the stuffing.

Making the namul
- Peel the *doraji* (bellflower roots) and cut into julienne strips. Rinse once with water to remove the sharp taste, then drain. Pan-fry together with minced spring onion and crushed garlic.
- Peel the *deodeok* (lance asiabell roots), julienne, then pan-fry with salt, minced spring onion and crushed garlic.
- Julienne the Korean radish and sauté in water. Season with salt and ginger juice, then cover with a lid and let it cook briefly. Add minced spring onion and crushed garlic, and stir-fry for a little longer.
- Slice the shiitake mushrooms into julienne strips and sauté in water. When the strips soften, add salt and sesame oil to finish.
- Cut the chestnuts into julienne strips, rinse well with water to remove the starch, and drain. Lightly toast in a pan.
- Season the clear beef broth with Korean soy sauce (*guk-ganjang*) and salt.
- Cut each abalone into three pieces and place them in a bowl. Top with the julienned, seasoned herbs. Carefully ladle the broth into the bowls, taking care not to disturb the arrangement.

전복꽃찜

SPRING

홍해삼
Honghaesam
Sea cucumber and mussel wrap

This delicate dish was traditionally served at ceremonies such as rituals and weddings in Gaeseong. Fresh sea cucumbers and mussels can be enjoyed raw, but they are also often dried for preservation. In particular, the flavour of red sea cucumbers intensifies and deepens through the process of drying, soaking and steaming. Minced meat and tofu are seasoned and rolled into meatballs, then wrapped with the sea cucumbers.

Ingredients
3 dried sea cucumbers
200 g (7 oz) dried Korean mussels
900 g (1 lb 15¾ oz) pork
200 g (7 oz) beef
400 g (14 oz) tofu
3 medium-sized eggs
2 tbsps starch powder
Korean soy sauce (*guk-ganjang*)
sesame oil

Seasoning for batter
1 tbsp Korean soy sauce
salt
⅔ tbsp sugar
1½ tbsps sesame oil
1 tbsp crushed garlic

Method
- Place the dried sea cucumbers in a pan, cover them with cold water, and heat gently. Turn off the heat just before the water reaches a rolling boil, and let the sea cucumbers cool in the water. Repeat this process twice a day for a week, changing the water each time. Over the course of the week, the sea cucumbers will soften and return to their original size. On the fifth day, split the belly of each sea cucumber and clean the inside thoroughly.
- Soak the dried mussels in little water.
- Slice the sea cucumbers in half lengthwise, season with soy sauce and sesame oil, and pan-fry until all the moisture disappears.
- Coat a pan with sesame oil and stir-fry the mussels.
- Finely grind the lean pork and beef using a grinder.
- Drain the tofu and press it through a fine sieve until smooth.
- Mix the pork, beef and tofu well, season the batter and knead.
- Roll out the batter thinly and place the stir-fried sea cucumber on top. Roll it into a ball. Repeat the same process for the mussels, stuffing them into meatballs.
- Cover the stuffed meat balls with starch powder and steam for about 8 minutes.
- Separate the eggs into whites and yolks, beat each well, and season with salt. Pour a thin layer of egg whites into a heated pan to make an omelette, then wrap the mussel-stuffed meatballs in it. Pour a thin layer of egg yolk into a heated pan to make an omelette, then wrap the sea cucumber-stuffed meatballs in it.
- Slice the stuffed omelettes neatly to serve.

SPRING

게찜
Ge-jjim
Steamed crab

Lee Gyubo, a writer from the Goryeo dynasty, enjoyed crab so much that he described crab broth as 'golden water'. Crab has long been a delicacy that stimulates the appetite, both then and now. To make this steamed crab dish, blue crab meat and roe are mixed with minced clam, mushroom, mung bean sprouts and tofu, then stuffed back into the crab shells. It is a dish thoughtfully prepared to be soft and easy to chew while preserving the full flavour and essence of crab.

Ingredients
3 fresh blue crabs
1 tbsp flour

Stuffing
80 g (2¾ oz) clam meat
3 shiitake mushrooms
½ onion
200 g (7 oz) mung bean sprouts
70 g (2½ oz) tofu
1 egg
10 g (⅓ oz) starch powder
salt
sesame oil
chopped spring onion (scallion)
crushed garlic

Method
- Deshell the fresh blue crabs by opening the shell from the back. Remove the gills and cut the crab in half. Carefully extract the roe and gently press to remove the lump meat.
- Wash the back shell thoroughly and let it dry.

Making the stuffing
- Rinse the clam meat in salted water and drain the water. Coat a heated pan with sesame oil and stir-fry the clam meat over a high heat without water.
- Slice the mushrooms into large pieces and toss them in a dry pan until they begin to soften and sweat. Add salt and sesame oil to finish.
- Coarsely chop the onion, sprinkle a little salt on it, drain any water and stir-fry.
- Remove the tails from the mung bean sprouts, add salt to boiling water, blanch quickly to keep them crunchy, drain the water and mix with sesame oil.
- Drain the tofu, mash it and season with salt.
- Put the prepared ingredients and the crab meat together, add beaten egg and starch powder, and mix well. The crab roe is carefully mixed in at the end.
- Sprinkle flour on the inside of the back shell, fill the prepared stuffing and steam in a preheated steamer for about 5 minutes.

활계찜
Hwalgye-jjim
Braised chicken with salted prawns

According to *Haedongjukji* (an old poetry book on seasonal customs), 'In Songdo, braised chicken is called *dori-tang*, and it is worth using decent *saeujeot* (fermented prawn/shrimp) to improve the taste', and, 'If you use sliced green chilli peppers generously and boil, it's also the best accompaniment to alcoholic drinks'. Seasoning with salted prawns (shrimp) is a distinctive feature of Gaeseong cuisine. Stir-fry the prawns over a high heat, then add the chicken. Pour in water and bring to a boil to create a savoury flavour while eliminating any fishy taste. *Dori-tang* tastes especially good when made with native Korean chicken.

Ingredients
1 chicken
2 potatoes
1 onion
5 shishito peppers
2 red chilli peppers
2 tbsps sesame oil
3 tbsps pounded *saeujeot* (fermented prawn/shrimp)
1 tsp grated ginger
2 tbsps minced spring onion (scallion)
1 tbsp crushed garlic

Method
- Cut the chicken into bite-sized pieces, then rinse thoroughly, making sure to clean between the bones. Drain well.
- Peel the potatoes, cut them into large pieces, and cut the onion into 4 equal parts.
- Remove the top of the shishito peppers. Cut the red chilli peppers on a bias.
- Heat sesame oil in a pan and stir-fry the *saeujeot* (fermented prawn/shrimp). Increase the heat to high and add the prepared chicken. When the chicken starts to brown, add the chopped potato and onion. Add the ginger and continue to sauté. Pour in enough water to just cover the ingredients.
- After boiling for about 15 minutes, add the shishito peppers, the red chilli peppers, the spring onion (scallion) and the garlic, and cook for another 10 minutes.

활계찜

SPRING

두부나물밥
Dubu-namul-bap
Rice with tofu and vegetables

The first recorded mention of tofu in Korean literature appears in the writings of Lee Saek, a scholar from the late Goryeo dynasty. He wrote, 'After eating only fresh vegetable soup for a long time, tofu tastes like slices of freshly boiled fat', and, 'Tofu fried in oil adds fragrance'. These records offer insight into the palate of the Goryeo people. At Onjium, tofu and *namul* rice is made by placing homemade, savoury tofu on top of rice cooked with thistle stalks grown on Ulleungdo Island.

Ingredients
360 g (2 cups) rice
500 g (1 lb 1⅝ oz) dried thistle stalks
300 g (10½ oz) tofu

Seasoning for namul
Korean soy sauce (*guk-ganjang*)
chopped spring onion (scallion)
crushed garlic
perilla oil

Tofu
400 g (14 oz) soybeans
100 g (3½ oz) unhulled pine nuts
2–3 tbsps coagulant

Method
- Rinse the rice thoroughly and soak in water for about 20 minutes.
- Blanch the thistle stalks in boiling salted water until soft. Cut into 2 cm (¾ in.) long slices and mix with the *namul* seasoning.
- Put the rice in a pot and start cooking. Once boiled, if the water evaporates, add the thistle *namul* and bring to a simmer.
- Put the rice in a bowl and add the tofu.

Making tofu
- Soak the soybeans in water for half a day. After soaking, grind them finely in a blender with the pine nuts. Transfer the mixture to a pot and bring to a boil. As soon as it comes to a boil, turn off the heat.
- Let the soybean juice cool slightly, then strain it through a muslin, squeezing to extract the liquid.
- Bring the soybean juice to a boil again. As froth forms, add a drop of perilla oil.
- Sprinkle the coagulant evenly over the soybean juice, then wait for the tofu to coagulate.
- Line a square mould with a cotton cloth, then pour in the soybean juice. Let the clear water drain and the tofu harden.

SPRING

게살무침밥
Ge-sal-muchim-bap
Rice with seasoned crab meat

Marinated blue crab, also known as *mujeot*, is a delicious dish. Onjium prepares *mujeot* and serves it atop freshly cooked white rice. To make the sauce, dried kelp (*dasima*) is added to Korean soy sauce (*guk-ganjang*), and the brine is brought to a boil. Then, plenty of chestnuts, dried dates (*jujubes*) and garlic strips are added to enrich the flavour. This sauce is then mixed with fresh crab meat to create a flavourful combination. The recipe makes a bountiful amount of sauce. Make the sauce 3–4 days in advance and use as often as needed.

Ingredients
360 g (2 cups) rice
700 g (1 lb 8¾ oz) fresh blue crab
300 g (10½ oz) northern prawns (shrimp)

Marinade
480 ml (2 cups) water
480 ml (2 cups) Korean soy sauce (*guk-ganjang*)
120 ml (½ cup) of *soju* (Korean hard liquor)
50 g (1¾ oz) dried kelp (*dasima*)
60 g (2 oz) sugar
50 g (1¾ oz) oligosaccharide syrup
4 tbsps Korean chilli powder
2 tbsps fine Korean chilli powder
100 g (3½ oz) chestnuts, sliced into thin strips
60 g (2 oz) dried Korean dates (*jujubes*), sliced into thin strips
80 g (2¾ oz) garlic, sliced into thin strips
30 g (1 oz) ginger, sliced into thin strips
chopped spring onion (scallion)
roasted sesame seeds

Method
- Wash the rice thoroughly and soak it in water for 20 minutes. Then, transfer it to a pan and begin cooking. Once it comes to a boil, reduce the heat and let it simmer.
- Deshell the fresh blue crabs by opening the shell from the back. Remove the gills and cut the crab in half. Carefully extract the roe and gently press to remove the lump meat.
- Peel the prawns (shrimp), rinse in mildly salted water and then drain water.

Making the sauce
- Add the water, the Korean soy sauce (*guk-ganjang*), the liquor and dried kelp (*dasima*), and bring to a boil. Lower the heat and simmer for a little longer, then remove the kelp.
- After cooling the brine, add the sugar, the oligosaccharide syrup and the chilli powder, and mix until thick.
- Add the strips of chestnuts, Korean dates (*jujubes*), garlic and ginger, and chopped spring onion (scallion). Sprinkle with the sesame seeds.
- Add 100g of the sauce to the crab meat and the prawns, mix well, and serve on top of the cooked rice.

SPRING

전복젓과 홍합해
Jeonbok-jeot and honghap-hae
Marinated abalone and mussels

Shipwrecks discovered off the coast of Taean, Chungcheongnam-do Province, contained clay jars filled with a variety of *jeotgal* (salted seafood), while a wooden strip listing details of 'salted seafood' such as salted crab, salted abalone and salted mussels was also found. This wooden strip served as an item list for shipping the *jeotgal* made in Jeolla-do Province, known for its high-quality seafood, to Gaeseong, the capital of the Goryeo dynasty. From this, we can infer the variety of salted seafood enjoyed by Gaeseong residents at the time. Onjium recommends salting abalone and mussels so that they can be enjoyed immediately.

Jeonbok-jeot (salted abalone)
1 kg (2 lb 4 oz) abalone (7 pieces)
3 tbsps coarse salt
200 g (7 oz) spring onion (scallion)
3 green chilli peppers
3 red chilli peppers
2 tbsps Korean chilli powder
2 tbsps Korean anchovy sauce
1 tbsp crushed garlic
roasted sesame seeds

Method
- Wash and trim the abalone. Remove the abalone from its shell and discard the innards. Score the abalone and slice thinly. Sprinkle with coarse salt for salting.
- Cut the spring onion (scallion) into 3 cm (1¼ in.) long slices. Cut the chilli pepper in half, deseed and cut on a bias.
- Add the Korean chilli powder, the fish sauce and the garlic to the marinated abalone. Mix well, then add the spring onion, the chilli peppers and the sesame seeds. Massage everything evenly into the abalone.

Honghap-hae (salted mussels)
1 kg (2 lb 4 oz) mussel meat
5 tbsps coarse salt
½ Korean radish
5 tbsps Korean chilli powder
100 g (3½ oz) spring onion
10 chestnuts
3 tbsps Korean anchovy sauce
3 tbsps starch syrup
2 tbsps crushed garlic
1 tbsp minced ginger
roasted sesame seeds

Method
- Trim the mussels, rinse them in mildly salted water, drain, and sprinkle with coarse salt.
- Cut the radish into 2 cm (¾ in.) wide and 4–5 cm (1½–2 in.) long thin rectangles and salt them. Drain water and mix with the Korean chilli powder.
- Cut the spring onions into 2 cm (¾ in.) long pieces and the chestnuts into slices.
- Add the Korean anchovy sauce, the starch syrup, the garlic, the ginger and the sesame seeds to the mussels and the radish. Mix well, then add the spring onion and the chestnuts, and mix evenly.

전복젓과 홍합해

SPRING

개성장땡이
Gaeseong-jangttaengi
Gaeseong dried pancakes

Jangttaengi is a traditional dish from the Gaeseong region. It is a type of pancake made by mixing minced meat with freshly made *doenjang* (fermented soybean paste), seasoning it, forming patties out of the mixture, and then drying. The pancakes are pan-fried before serving. The savoury depth of the *doenjang*, combined with the rich flavour of the meat, delivers a deep, umami-packed taste. This fermented dish is quite different from those commonly eaten these days. With its combination of meat and seasoning, along with the drying and fermentation process, it develops a salami-like texture, making it an ideal side dish or accompaniment to alcoholic beverages. It is intended to be preserved and eaten over time. The method is the same for each of the meat pancakes.

Sogogi jangttaengi (beef pancake)

100 g (¾ cup) glutinous rice flour
50 g (⅓ cup) sorghum flour
50 g (1¾ oz) freshly made *doenjang* (fermented soybean paste)
200 g (7 oz) beef
1 green chilli pepper
1 red chilli pepper
1½ tbsps minced spring onion (scallion)
1 tbsp crushed garlic

Dwaejigogi jangttaengi (pork pancake)

100 g (¾ cup) glutinous rice flour
50 g (⅓ cup) sorghum flour
50 g (1¾ oz) freshly made *doenjang*
200 g (7 oz) pork
1 green chilli pepper
1 red chilli pepper
1½ tbsps minced spring onion
1 tbsp crushed garlic

Sogogi and dwaejigogi jangttaengi (beef and pork pancake)

100 g (¾ cup) glutinous rice flour
50 g (⅓ cup) sorghum flour
50 g (1¾ oz) freshly made *doenjang*
200 g (7 oz) beef
200 g (7 oz) pork
1 green chilli pepper
1 red chilli pepper
1½ tbsps minced spring onion
1 tbsp crushed garlic

Method
- Put the glutinous rice flour, the sorghum flour and the freshly made *doenjang* (fermented soybean paste) together and mix well.
- Mince the meat.
- Cut the chilli peppers in half, deseed and finely chop.
- Add the chopped chilli peppers, spring onion (scallion) and garlic to the meat and mix well.
- Mix the meat with the combined glutinous rice flour, sorghum flour and the freshly made *doenjang*.
- Form patties from the mixture, place them on a tray with holes, and allow them to dry in a well-ventilated area for about a day.
- Steam in a bamboo steamer for 10 minutes, then allow the water to evaporate.
- Once well dried, place the patties in a vacuum-sealed pack and store them in the freezer. Take out only the amount needed when ready to eat.
- Just before serving, sear in a hot pan or lightly grill. Slice and place on a plate.

Dishes of Onjium: Korean Food of Nature and Formality

Jeong Hye Gyeong
Director of Onjium Food Studio

Left:
Geon-jeonbok (dried abalone)

It is gratifying to see young chefs experimenting with Korean cuisine in new and innovative ways. However, I believe that the more people experiment with Korean food and push the boundaries of tradition, the more its spirit, philosophy and unique nature seem to be lost. While global interest in Korean food will undoubtedly continue to grow, the concern arises: how much can the cuisine evolve before it loses its distinct identity? If that happens, can it still truly be called Korean food?

Onjium is a cultural space dedicated to the exploration of Korean cuisine and its broader cultural context. The researchers aim to discover the archetype of traditional Korean food and reinterpret it for the modern age, right here in Seoul. But what exactly defines Korean food, and in which direction should Onjium go? These are complex questions that cannot be answered simply. However, I will explore the taste and spirit of Korean cuisine that Onjium seeks to preserve by examining its identity and unique traditions.

The Harmony of Five: Colours, Tastes, Elements, Seasons and Garnishes in Cosmological Cuisine
Korean food encompasses the entirety of the universe. Even a single dish is rich with diverse colours, ingredients, garnishes of every kind and all sorts of spices. Rooted in Eastern cosmism, which is based on the principles of Yin-Yang and the Five Elements theory, Korean food reflects a deep philosophical connection to balance and harmony. This approach does not prioritize one ingredient or flavour over another; rather, it seeks a harmonious blend of all elements. At first glance, Korean food may seem chaotic, but in reality, each dish embodies the principles of the universe. For example, Korean cuisine emphasizes the balance between yin and yang, that is, the harmony between plant-based and animal-sourced ingredients. Even salted seafood, an essential component of *kimchi* – the quintessential Korean vegetable dish – contributes to its complex, fermented flavour. Based on the Five Elements (wood, fire, earth, metal and water), Korean cooking incorporates five grains, five types of livestock (beef, lamb, pork, poultry and, historically, dog meat), and five fruits to create five colours and five tastes. This belief in balance extends to the philosophy that the 'roots of medicine and food are the same (藥食同源)', where food is not only nourishment but also a form of holistic wellbeing.

The Koreans have long regarded the five fundamental tastes – sourness, bitterness, pungency, sweetness and saltiness – as essential to their cuisine, with the harmony of these five tastes to be of the utmost importance. Unlike Western cuisine, which sees pungency as algesia rather than a taste, Korean cuisine includes pungency as an integral part of the flavour spectrum. The subtle taste of fermentation reveals itself gradually as these five tastes blend harmoniously, and can be said to be the essence of the five tastes.

Korean cuisine also places great emphasis on colour sense, maintaining a balance of five key colours – red, blue, yellow, white and black – in mind. Of these, black and white are especially significant. The use of empty space was regarded as a space of white, while egg whites were often separated to serve as white garnishes. Black ingredients, such as black sesame and rock mushrooms, are used meaningfully in diverse ways. While Western cuisine traditionally avoided the inclusion of black in dishes, black ingredients are now gaining in popularity, highlighting the sophisticated colour sensibility inherent in traditional Korean cuisine.

Korean cuisine emphasizes the balanced use of five grains (rice, barley, corn, millet and sorghum), five fruits (peach, plum, apricot, chestnut and Korean dates or *jujubes*) and five meats in equal measure, ensuring that no one ingredient dominates. Harmony in taste is of utmost importance, with a focus on balance rather than reliance on any single flavour. Unlike Western cuisine, which tends to focus on the dichotomy of hot and cold temperatures, Korean cuisine classifies food temperature into five categories (cold, hot, warm, cool and calm) and applies these to the balance of tastes. This is reflected in the Korean expression 'it's cool', which is used even after consuming a hot dish, which originates from this unique approach to food temperature.

Harmony of season and taste are also considered important in Korean cuisine. The Koreans believed that the ideal flavours should align with the seasons: more sourness in spring dishes, bitterness in summer dishes, pungency in autumn and more saltiness in winter dishes. The human body feels lassitude after the long winter and needs vitamins, so sour-tasting spring vegetables were seen as a restorative herbal medicine. During the hot summer months, when appetite wanes, bitter-tasting herbs such as ginseng, Korean angelica root and mugwort were used to restore vitality. In autumn, pungent ingredients that raise body temperature were used to infuse the human body with warm energy in preparation for the long winter to come. Finally, in the dry and severe winter, saltiness was favoured to encourage the uptake of water to the body and maintain the body's balance.

Korean cuisine is renowned for its artful use of garnishes, which are not only visually striking but also serve to stimulate the appetite. Nowhere else in the world are dishes adorned with such exquisite and meaningful decorations. Take eggs, for example – a universal ingredient. In Korean cooking, eggs are transformed into vibrant garnishes by separating the yolk and egg white to represent the yellow and white from the traditional Korean colour spectrum, *obangsaek* (the five colours). Beyond eggs, a variety of natural ingredients are used to achieve this colourful harmony, including red pepper strips, pine nuts, manna lichen (a rare type of rock mushroom) and *minari* (Korean watercress). In Korean cuisine, the principle of garnishing is to express *obangsaek* using colours derived from natural ingredients, finishing each dish with a harmonious balance of red, blue, yellow, white and black. This thoughtful approach elevates garnishing from mere decoration to an essential part of the dish's identity.

The Philosophy of Seasoning

Seasoning is at the heart of Korean cuisine, and no Korean would think twice about adding staples such as green onion (scallion), garlic, ginger and sesame oil to a dish. While seasoning is fundamental to Korean food, its deeper significance has often been overlooked. A closer look at the Korean word for seasoning, *yangnyeom*, reveals the cultural and philosophical roots behind this practice.

The term *yangnyeom* is composed of the two syllables: *yang* (meaning 'medicine') and *nyeom* (meaning 'thinking'). This connection reflects the age-old Korean belief that seasoning food requires the same thoughtful approach as preparing medicine. In this tradition, seasoning is not just about enhancing flavour – it is about nurturing the body and restoring balance.

In contrast, the history of Western cuisine is often intertwined with the development of spices, valued for their ability to add taste and aroma to dishes. While spices in the West are primarily used for flavour, Korean seasonings are carefully chosen for their medicinal and restorative properties, as well as their culinary roles. For Koreans, food has always been more than just sustenance – it is medicine to nourish both the human body and soul.

Ritual and Seasonal Foods

Influenced by Confucianism, Koreans have long placed great importance on rituals in their everyday life, and this cultural value is deeply reflected in their cuisine. Ritual meals have evolved to mark every major rite of passage in life, with special table settings designed for celebrations such as a baby's 100th day, a first birthday, coming-of-age ceremonies, weddings and one's sixtieth birthday. The table setting, called the *gobaesang* or 'table of high piles' – a table piled high with an abundance of food – stands out as especially representative of Korean culture. This tradition continues today, and the heavily laden table is set not only for memorial rituals and ancestral rites but for joyous celebrations such as weddings and milestone birthday parties.

Table settings for the celebration of each season were also an integral part of Korean life, with tables featuring different seasonal foods that turned each occasion into a joyous event. While industrialization and urbanization have brought significant change, the practice of honouring the seasons through food, products of an agrarian society, remains central to Korean culture, especially during traditional festive holidays such as the Lunar New Year and *Chuseok* (Korean Thanksgiving).

Believing that consuming seasonal foods restores health, Koreans have long tailored their diets to align with nature's cycles. In spring, when fresh vegetables were scarce during the winter, they embraced the freshly collected vegetables of the first harvest to rejuvenate their bodies. During the hot summer months, dishes like *samgyetang* (ginseng chicken soup) and *yukgaejang* (spicy beef and vegetable soup) were enjoyed to boost stamina. Autumn brought bowls of newly harvested

rice and fresh fruits, and when winter approached, large quantities of *kimchi* were prepared for a period when fresh vegetables would be hard to come by. In essence, Koreans long ago developed seasonal foods as a way to harmonize with nature rather than work against it. Korean cuisine follows the rhythms and principles of nature, a philosophy that Onjium deeply values and aspires to preserve for future generations.

The Science of Fermentation and Preservation in Korean Cuisine

Vegetables and fermented foods form the cornerstone of Korean cuisine. Rooted in the understanding that each and every food ingredient can be found in nature, Koreans have developed an extensive range of vegetarian recipes and fermented foods. Among these dishes, *kimchi* stands out as the most iconic – a fermented vegetable dish preserved through a unique method. Other typical fermented Korean foods include *jang* (sauces) of all kinds such as soy sauce, *doenjang* (fermented soybean paste) and *gochujang* (red pepper paste), alongside, of course, traditional Korean alcoholic beverages.

While fermentation is done all over the world, Korean cuisine distinguishes itself by focusing on vegetable-based fermentation, as can be seen in *kimchi* and *jang*. In contrast to fermented dairy, meat and fish products in other countries, such as cheese, yoghurt and raw fermented ham in the West, or fish sauce in Southeast Asia, Korea's approach prioritizes vegetables. Korean *jang* is integral to countless dishes. For example, healthy vegetable dishes are seasoned with *jang*; the classic marinated grilled beef dish *bulgogi* relies on *jang* for flavour; and Korean pickles collectively called *jangajji* are made by salting vegetables in *jang*.

At Onjium, this rich tradition of fermentation and preservation unique to Korean cuisine is celebrated and further developed, ensuring these techniques continue to evolve and expand the horizon and depth of Korean cuisine.

Onjium: Preserving the Essence of Traditional Korean Cuisine

Unusual full-course Korean meals, often presented as traditional or modern, are becoming increasingly popular as Korean food gains global attention. However, this trend is a concern to us at Onjium, since many of these meals lack the basics of true Korean cuisine. Korean cuisine is an integral part of the cultural heritage of the Korean people passed down for thousands of years, deeply rooted in formality and etiquette. We at Onjium, therefore, deeply considered the essence of truly Korean foods and arrived at the conclusion that they are best represented by the cuisine of the nobility in Seoul, the capital of the Joseon dynasty for over five hundred years. Onjium is committed to upholding the philosophy and spirit of this noble cuisine as the core of our culinary approach.

The cuisine of Seoul's nobility placed great importance on formality and etiquette. What set it apart was not the number of side dishes, the types of recipes or the complexity of preparation, but the culinary spirit behind the food. This spirit involves preparing dishes with the utmost care and sincerity out of love for ancestors and family, even when using only a very tiny portion of red pepper or ground sesame. The Korean nobility handed down a culinary tradition characterized by simplicity, great discipline and sincerity, avoiding extravagance in their table settings.

Onjium has preserved and honoured this tradition by recreating the essence of noble Seoul cuisine. The taste we aspire to is 'fresh, plain, delicious and simple'. This is exactly the same taste that was sought by the nobility in Seoul. For example, soup and *kimchi* were served at every meal of the Joseon nobility. The soup was always clear and free of fat, while *kimchi* was prepared simply with salted prawns (shrimp) or even soy sauce instead of adding salted fish, creating a light and refreshing flavour. Influenced by royal cuisine, the nobility, in some respects, valued intricate and precise recipes, through which they tried to attain ultimately nothing but the taste inherent to the ingredients. In essence, they aspired to achieve a 'truly natural taste', despite the fact that the ingredients underwent the 'cultural process' of 'cooking'. Inspired by this philosophy, Onjium aspires to craft dishes that contain the tastes of the ingredients as they undergo careful cooking procedures.

Onjium will continue to create Korean dishes that taste refreshing, simple and authentic, highlighting the natural flavours inherent in each ingredient. Korean cuisine embodies nature while embracing formality.

Through meticulous care, consideration and etiquette, the laws of nature transform into ambrosial sustenance, beautifully presented at the table. Onjium strives to create a modern table setting that honours both contemporary tastes and the uniqueness of Korean food. This is the taste of today that Onjium is determined to create, and this is the Korean food of today that Onjium is committed to preserve.

Left:
Dureup (fatsia shoot)

Previous page:
Goryeo celadon bowl

Following page:
River pufferfish (*hwang-bok*)

여름

SUMMER

may grow green and thick

SUMMER

단새우물회
Dan-saewu-mul-hwe
Raw sweet prawn soup

Inspired by a specialty of Nohwa-do Island, in which a clear raw abalone soup is prepared without adding red chilli pepper paste or vinegar, Onjium has created a raw sweet prawn (shrimp) soup using frozen tomato juice made from fresh tomatoes. Prawns, abalones and vegetables are mixed with frozen tomato juice and served cold.

Ingredients
200 g (7 oz) of sweet prawns (shrimps), skinned and heads removed
2 abalones
½ stalk of spring onion (scallion)
1 cucumber, finely shredded
½ Korean pear
50 g (1¾ oz) dried *parae* (green laver seaweed)
1 tomato
cheongju (Korean rice wine)

Tomato juice
4 tomatoes
sugar (30% of total tomato weight)

Method
- To make the tomato juice, peel the tomatoes and cut each tomato into 8 pieces. Mix with sugar and crush the tomatoes by hand to release the juices. Strain the crushed tomatoes through a large sieve and allow the juice to drain for about 12 hours to achieve a clear consistency. Freeze the juice.
- Clean the prawns (shrimp) in salted water. Pat dry with a paper towel.
- Place the abalone shell-side down in a basket set over boiling water. Drizzle *cheongju* (Korean rice wine) over them. Top with the spring onion (scallion) and steam for 1½ hours. Remove the abalone meat from shells. Cut into 3 or 4 pieces.
- Briefly soak the dried *parae* (green laver seaweed) in water.
- Rinse the shredded cucumber in cold water and strain. Peel the pear and cut into wedges. Peel the tomato and cut into 8 wedges.
- Place the frozen tomato juice at the centre of a plate and arrange the other prepared ingredients around it. As the tomato juice melts, this becomes a cool seafood soup.

단새우물회
Dan-saewu-mul-hwe

SUMMER

밀쌈
Mil-ssam
Stick roll

Mil-ssam, a traditional Korean dish, is made by rolling thinly julienned ingredients like cucumber, mushrooms and meat in delicate wheat flour pancakes. This healthy, nutritious and visually appealing food can be enhanced with vibrant colour variations in the dough by adding spinach or *buchu* (wild chives). Sometimes, a single large roll is made and then sliced into bite-sized pieces.

Filling
100 g (3½ oz) beef bottom sirloin,
    cut into 4 cm (1½ in.) matchsticks
4 dried shiitake mushrooms
1 cucumber, seeded and cut into 4 cm (1½ in.) matchsticks
60 g (2 oz) carrot, cut into 4 cm (1½ in.) matchsticks
100 g (3½ oz) white radish, cut into 4 cm (1½ in.) matchsticks
100 g (3½ oz) mung bean sprouts, heads and tails removed
salt
sesame oil

Seasoning for beef and shiitake
soy sauce
sugar
chopped spring onion (scallion)
minced garlic
sesame oil
roasted sesame seeds
pepper

Batter for crepes
200 g (1⅔ cups) flour plus 2 tbsps flour for spinach crepes
400 ml (1⅔ cups) water
salt
2 tbsps spinach juice

Mustard sauce
2 tbsps mustard powder
1 tbsp water
1 tbsp vinegar
1 tsp sugar
1 tbsp Korean pear juice
salt
soy sauce

Method
- Soak the shiitake in water for 2 hours. Cut off the stems and shred. Season the shiitake and beef separately. Stir-fry separately.
- Soak the cucumber in lightly salted water for 20 minutes. Squeeze out the excess water. Stir-fry. Blanch the carrots in boiling water. Season with salt. Stir-fry. Soak the white radish in lightly salted water for 20 minutes. Strain and stir-fry. Parboil the bean sprouts.
- Make mustard sauce. Mix mustard powder with warm water. Let stand for 2 hours. When it turns dark, dries and cracks, pour in hot water. Let stand for a while to remove the stringency and strain. Add vinegar, sugar, pear juice, a dash of salt, and soy sauce and mix well.
- Make the batter for the crepes. Add a dash of salt to the flour. Mix equal parts flour and water to form the batter, then divide it into 2 equal portions. Add spinach juice and 2 tbsps of flour to one of the portions. Add oil to a pan and heat over a medium heat. Ladle in the batter to form small crepes and cook until crisp, about 1 minute.
- Mix the sautéed ingredients and mung bean sprouts. Add salt to taste. Mix with sesame oil and mustard sauce.
- Place a small amount of filling at the centre of each crepe and roll tight.

어교순대
Eogyo soondae
Soondae stuffed in a croaker's air bladder

Croaker, a sweet-flavoured fish best enjoyed in summer, is known for its invigorating properties and benefits for bone health. A seasonal delicacy, this version of *soondae* (Korean sausage) is made by steaming the croaker's gelatin-rich air bladder, which is stuffed with a mixture of seasoned beef, bean curd and bean sprouts. The soft yet chewy texture of the air bladder combined with the flavourful stuffing creates the perfect balance in this unique fish sausage.

Ingredients
air bladder of croaker
100 g (3½ oz) beef, minced
3 dried shiitake mushrooms
50 g (1¾ oz) tofu
70 g (2½ oz) mung bean sprouts
70 g (2½ oz) onion, chopped
30 g (1 oz) *minari* (Korean watercress)
salt
flour

Seasoning for beef and shiitake
soy sauce
sugar
chopped spring onion (scallion)
crushed garlic
sesame oil
roasted sesame seeds
pepper

Method
- Remove the fat and blood from the air bladder. Be careful not to make a hole in it.
- Soak the shiitake mushrooms in water for 2 hours. Strain and shred. Season the shiitake and beef. Mash the tofu and squeeze out excess water. Blanch mung bean sprouts. Chop and squeeze out excess water. Stir-fry the onion. Blanch the *minari* (Korean watercress) in boiling water. Rinse in cold water and squeeze out excess water and chop. Mix all filling ingredients and season with salt.
- Sprinkle the inside of the air bladder with flour and squeeze the filling into the bladder. Stick a skewer at the end of the bladder to prevent the filling from poking out.
- Steam the stuffed bladder in a basket set over boiling water for about 10 minutes.
- Cut into rounds just before serving.

SUMMER

사슬적
Saseul-jeok
Beef and fish skewers

The name of this dish in Korean is *saseul-jeok*, derived from *saseul*, meaning 'chain' in Korean, as its preparation involves grilling beef and fish alternately skewered like a chain. Fresh, seasonal fish is used, with croaker in the summer and cod in the winter. Nutritious and aesthetically pleasing, this dish is a great alternative to an all-meat dish. Pan-frying finely minced beef makes the beef taste softer and more flavourful.

Ingredients
400 g (14 oz) croaker fillet
300 g (10½ oz) sirloin strip, finely shredded
4–5 skewers

Seasoning for fish
1 tsp Korean soy sauce (*guk-ganjang*)
1 tbsp Korean pear juice
1 tbsp perilla seed oil

Seasoning for beef
1 tbsp soy sauce
⅔ tbsp sugar
⅔ tbsp chopped spring onion (scallion)
½ tbsp crushed garlic
2 tbsps chopped onion
1 tbsp chopped pear
1 tsp roasted sesame seeds
1 tsp sesame oil
pepper
starch

Method
- Cut the fish into pieces 8 cm (3⅛ in.) long and 1.5 cm (⅝ in.) thick. Marinate in fish seasoning.
- Mix the beef with the beef seasoning. Divide into pieces just like the fish.
- Skewer the fish and beef alternately.
- Place paper foil on the grate. Put the skewers on the foil and grill both sides.
- Remove the skewers and plate the food before serving.

사슬적

여름 편육
Yeoreum pyeonyuk
Slices of boiled meat

Pyeonyuk is a traditional Korean dish consisting of thinly sliced meat that has been boiled until tender. It showcases the unique and flavourful ways Koreans prepare healthy meat dishes. This particular recipe for *pyeonyuk* has been passed down through generations by the Heo family clan in Jisu-myeon, Gyeongsangnam-do.

Ingredients
500 g (1 lb 5⁄8 oz) pork belly
500 g (1 lb 5⁄8 oz) pork shoulder
1 stalk of spring onion (scallion), finely shredded

Ingredients to be boiled
5 garlic cloves
1 spring onion
½ onion
1 tsp ginger
10 peppercorns
1 dried red pepper
1 tbsp *doenjang* (fermented soybean paste)
salt

Method
- Soak the pork in water for about 10 hours to remove blood. Plunge the pork in boiling water and take out immediately.
- In a large covered pan, add all the ingredients to be boiled and bring to a boil for 10 minutes. Add the pork and boil for another 45 to 50 minutes.
- When the pork is cooked, remove from the pan. Wrap the pork in a clean cotton cloth and press it down with a heavy weight for a few hours to shape into a neat loaf. Cut the meat into thin slices.
- Rinse the spring onion (scallion) in cold water. Strain well.
- Arrange the meat slices on a plate with the shredded spring onion on the side.

연저육찜
Yeonjeoyuk-jjim
Braised pork

This is a special dish featuring tender pork, prepared through a somewhat complex process involving boiling, pan-frying and braising in seasonings. However, the delicate, tender flavour makes the effort well worth it. The dish also combines both pork and beef, allowing everyone to enjoy the richness of both meats. Skinned green grapes make the perfect garnish, adding a refreshing touch to this summer dish.

Ingredients
500 g (1 lb 1⅝ oz) pork belly
200 g (7 oz) pork neck
200 g (7 oz) beef sirloin
5 dried Korean dates (*jujubes*), seeded
10 ginkgo nuts, skinned
10 green grapes, skinned
1 tbsp starch

Seasoning for pork
100 ml (⅖ cup) soy sauce
3 tbsps starch syrup
2 tbsps muscovado sugar
240 ml (1 cup) beef brisket broth
100 ml (⅖ cup) Korean pear juice
1 tsp peppercorns
5 cloves of garlic
½ cheongyang green pepper
¼ onion
1 knob of ginger

Method
- Soak the pork in cold water to remove blood. Strain well. Add peppercorns to boiling water. Put the meat in the boiling water and cook for 40 minutes. Add oil to a pan. Grill the pork in the pan until it is golden brown.
- Peel the skins of the Korean dates (*jujubes*) into thin, rolling sheets and cut each date into 3 pieces. Crack open the shells of the ginkgo nuts and remove the thin membranes.
- Mix all pork seasoning ingredients. Boil for 10 minutes. Add the grilled pork and beef to the seasoning and braise for 20 minutes over a low heat.
- Scoop out 100 ml (⅖ cup) of the seasoning liquid to make the sauce. Add the dried Korean dates, ginkgo nuts and grapes, and cook for 10 minutes over a low heat. Add the starch to thicken the sauce at the end.
- Slice the pork and beef. Arrange on a plate. Drizzle with the sauce.

SUMMER

장어밥
Jangeo-bap
Rice with eel

Rice cooked with eel is just as satisfying and delicious as grilled eel. Onjium's eel rice, prepared with eel stock made from the backbones and fins of the eel, is a seasonal delicacy. Eel fillets contain many tiny, thin edible bones, but making fine slashes in the eel cuts the bones into small pieces, making the fillet easier to eat. The eel is then boiled in salted water, resulting in a wonderfully moist and tender fish fillet.

Ingredients
360 g (2 cups) rice
2 eels
2 eggs (to make ribbons for garnish)
20 g (¾ oz) chopped spring onion (scallion)
salt

Eel stock
30 g (1 oz) dried kelp (*dasima*)
2 dried red peppers
1 tbsp peppercorns
10 g (⅓ oz) *gamcho* (liquorice root)

Method
- Soak the rice in water for 30 minutes.
- Skin the eels with the blade of a knife and rub salt into the skin of the eel to remove the slippery coating. Make fine slashes in the eel to cut through the tiny bones in the fillet. Boil the eel in salted water, then cut into bite-sized pieces.
- Grill the backbone, head and fins of the eel. Put them into 2 L (2 qts ½ cup) of water together with the stock ingredients. Boil for about 1 hour on a low heat. When the stock begins to boil, remove the kelp (*dasima*).
- Put the rice in the eel stock. Bring to a boil. Turn the heat to low and continue to cook for 10 minutes. Add the eel and simmer for another 10 minutes.
- Separate the egg yolks and whites. Cook each into a thin omelette. Cut into ribbon-like strips.
- When the rice is cooked, garnish with the thin egg ribbons and chopped spring onion (scallion).

SUMMER

백육개장
Baek-yukgaejang
Mild beef and vegetable soup

This soup is smoky, spicy and rich, featuring hearty hunks of sliced beef and plenty of vegetables that are tender yet retain their earthy mountain flavour from *gosari* (bracken). Served with rice, it makes for a satisfying, warming meal. Based on the traditional recipe for spicy beef and vegetable soup known as *yukgaejang*, Onjium offers a less spicy but richly flavoured soup without hot pepper powder. This recipe yields 7–8 servings.

Ingredients
500 g (1 lb 1⅝) beef brisket
30 g (1 oz) piece of dried kelp (*dasima*)
600 g (1 lb 5⅛ oz) *yang* (large cow intestines)
300 g (10½ oz) *gopchang* (small cow intestines)
70 g (2½ oz) *toran* (taro)*
50 g (1¾ oz) dried *gosari* (bracken)
1 spring onion (scallion)
2 tbsps *doenjang* (fermented soybean paste)
peppercorns
minced garlic
Korean soy sauce (*guk-ganjang*)
salt

Method
- To make the beef brisket broth, first soak the beef brisket in water for about 1 hour to draw out the blood. In a pot, add plenty of water, the beef and the kelp (*dasima*). Simmer for 1½ hours, removing the kelp after 30 minutes. Remove the meat and tear it along the grain into strips.
- Remove the fat from the *gopchang* (small cow intestines). Dip it briefly in boiling water. Bring 2 L (2 qts ½ cup) of fresh water to a boil. Add the *yang* (large cow intestines), *gopchang*, *doenjang* (fermented soybean paste) and peppercorns. Boil for 2 hours. Set aside 240 ml (1 cup) of the liquid.
- Soak the *toran* (taro) and *gosari* (bracken) in water. Strain and boil until tender. Strain and cut into 5 cm (2 in.) long pieces. Cut the spring onion (scallion) into 5 cm (2 in.) long pieces and rinse in cold water to remove the sticky sap.
- Add 240 ml (1 cup) of the *yang* and *gopchang* broth to boiled water reserved for the beef brisket broth. Add the beef strips, *yang*, *gopchang*, *toran* and *gosari*. Boil for 20 minutes. Add the spring onion. Put the finely minced garlic in a sieve and brew it in the beef brisket broth.
- When all the ingredients are well cooked, season the stock with Korean soy sauce (*guk-ganjang*) and salt.

* *Toran* is a Korean root vegetable, similar to a yam but less sweet.

SUMMER

냉면
Naengmyeon
Cold noodles

Cold noodles in icy broth, called *naengmyeon* in Korean, are especially refreshing on a hot summer day. The broth is made from a combination of fermented *dongchimi* brine and beef stock. Topped with slices of beef, pear and cucumber, these icy cold noodles in a chilled broth are savoury and offer perfect relief from the summer heat. This recipe yields 6 servings.

Ingredients
600 g (1 lb 5⅛ oz) beef brisket
30 g (1 oz) piece of kelp (*dasima*)
1.2 L (5 cups) *dongchimi* (white radish water *kimchi*) liquid
salt
sugar
vinegar
1 white radish from *dongchimi*
1½ cucumbers
½ pear, peeled, cored and thinly sliced lengthwise
2 eggs
600 g (1 lb 5⅛ oz) noodles
crushed garlic
sesame oil

Seasoning for the dongchimi
Korean soy sauce (*guk-ganjang*)
salt
vinegar
sugar
ground red pepper
minced garlic

Method
- To make the beef brisket broth, first soak the beef brisket in water for about 1 hour to draw out the blood. In a pot, add plenty of water, the beef and the kelp (*dasima*). Simmer for 1½ hours, removing the kelp after 30 minutes.
- Remove the meat and wrap it in paper towels. Place something heavy on top of the meat to keep it flat. Slice the brisket into thin slices. Strain the beef broth through a muslin.
- Add the *dongchimi* liquid to 1.2 L (5 cups) beef broth. Season with salt, sugar and vinegar. Keep refrigerated until very cold. Slice a well-fermented *dongchimi* radish into thin squares. Mix with *dongchimi* seasoning.
- Cut the cucumber lengthwise into slices. Soak in salted water for 10 minutes, being careful not to soak too long to keep it crispy. Rinse in cold water. Squeeze out excess water and season with crushed garlic and sesame oil.
- Separate the egg yolks and whites. Cook each into a thin omelette. Cut into ribbons for yellow and white garnish.
- Cook the noodles in boiling water until the noodles are chewy. Strain and rinse with cold water.
- Place the noodles in a large bowl. Top with the beef slices, seasoned *dongchimi* radish, cucumber, pear and egg ribbons. Pour the chilled broth over the pile of noodles in the bowl.

SUMMER

밀천신
Mil-cheonsin
Chicken and bellflower root wrap

Every Yudujeol, 15 June of the lunar calendar, ancient Koreans held ceremonies to pray for a good harvest to their ancestor gods and the God of Farming. For the ceremony, they prepared noodles, crepe-like *jeonbyeong* and bowls of *tteok* strips in honey made from fresh wheat or barley, offering them alongside seasonal Korean melons and watermelons. The ceremony was called *Yudu-cheonsin*, and *Mil-cheonsin* refers to the wheat crepes prepared for the occasion. Chicken broth is added to the batter for the crepes, and the chicken meat, mixed with *doraji-namul* (cooked bellflower root), is wrapped inside.

Ingredients
1 whole small chicken, or 1 kg (2 lb 4 oz) chicken cuts with bones
dried kelp (*dasima*)
500 g (1 lb 1⅝ oz) *doraji* (bellflower root)
1 tbsp minced spring onion (scallion)
1 tsp crushed garlic
salt
hot mustard sauce

For the wheat crepe batter
100 g (3½ oz) lean beef cut
20 g (¾ oz) tofu
4 medium-sized eggs
5 rock ear mushrooms (*seogi-beoseot*)
50 g (1¾ oz) water celery
100 g (3½ oz) cod fillet

Making the filling
- Rinse the chicken clean and cut into 4 pieces. Put the dried kelp (*dasima*) and water in a pan, boil for about 30 minutes, then remove the chicken and kelp.
- Separate the chicken meat from the bones. Return the bones to the broth and boil for another 20 minutes. Strain the broth through a fine sieve and chill.
- Shred the meat and season lightly with salt.
- Peel the *doraji* (bellflower roots) and cut into julienne strips. Rinse once with water to remove the sharp taste, drain and sauté. Add minced spring onions (scallions) and crushed garlic, and season with salt while stir-frying.
- Add hot mustard sauce to the chicken meat and pan-fried *doraji*, then mix.

Making the wheat crepes
- Finely chop the rock ear mushrooms (*seogi-beoseot*), soaked in water.
- Pour the chicken broth into the flour, add the beaten egg, and mix in the rock ear mushrooms to make the batter.
- Heat a frying pan, brushed with a little oil, and spread the batter evenly just to cover the bottom of the frying pan to make the crepes.
- Place the mixture of chicken meat and *doraji* in the centre of each crepe and roll into a wrap.

밀천신

SUMMER

오이선
Oi-seon
Chilled cucumber with beef broth

One of the royal kitchen's go-to dishes was *seon* – steamed, stuffed bite-sized vegetables. *Oi-seon* is an early summertime dish made with mellow young cucumbers, stuffed with beef, steamed, and served in clear, cold broth. It was a signature summer offering for guests in Gaeseong. Many defectors from Gaeseong say its simple, yet refreshing taste is what they miss most from home.

Ingredients
7 Korean cucumbers, thin and mellow
100 g (3½ oz) lean beef cut
beef marinade (*see *Okjamhwa-kkot-ssam*, page 148)
starch powder
480 ml (2 cups) beef broth
salt
a few pine nuts

For the beef broth
1 kg (2 lb 4 oz) of brisket
6 L (6¼ qts) of water
dried kelp (*dasima*)

Making the beef broth
Sit the brisket in cold water to draw out blood, then blanch in boiling water and drain. Put water, the blanched brisket and dried kelp (*dasima*) into a pot and bring to a boil. Skim off any foam to keep the broth clear. Remove the dried kelp after 30 minutes and continue boiling the brisket for 1 more hour.

Method
- Slice cucumbers into 3 cm (1¼ in.) thick circles. Make 2 cm (¾ in.) deep cross-shaped cuts on one side of each circle to make a half-opening, then sprinkle with salt. Let sit for about 30 minutes until the cuts open slightly.
- Mince the beef by hand and marinate in the sauce.
- Stuff the beef into the cucumber openings and dust with starch powder.
- Place the stuffed cucumbers in a heated steamer and cook for about 3 minutes. Immediately chill the cucumbers in ice water and drain.
- Chill the clear beef broth.
- Place the stuffed cucumbers in a bowl and pour over the cold broth. Garnish with pine nuts.

칼싹두기
Kalssakdugi
Hand-cut noodle soup

Kalssakdugi is a type of *kalguksu* (hand-cut noodle) made with buckwheat dough rolled thin and cut into finger-width strips. The dish gets its name from *kal*, meaning 'knife' in Korean because the dough is cut with a knife. The noodles are boiled in broth and served with meat and *kimchi*, seasoned with sauce.

Ingredients
1 *aehobak* (a type of Korean summer squash) or courgette (zucchini)
100 g (3½ oz) lean beef cut
beef marinade (*see *Okjamhwa-kkot-ssam*, page 148)
⅓ head of *kimchi* cabbage
salt
1.9 L (2 qts) beef broth
Korean soy sauce (*guk-ganjang*)

Preparing the dough
180 g (1½ cups) buckwheat flour
60 g (½ cup) wheat flour
5 to 6 tbsps water
salt

Method
- Make the dough by mixing buckwheat flour, wheat flour and a bit of salt, and kneading with hot water. Roll it thin, then cut into 2 cm (¾ in.) thick noodles.
- Chop the *aehobak* (Korean summer squash) into 4 cm (1½ in.) long blocks, peel each block into one long sheet (*dolryeokkaki*), then julienne. Sprinkle with a bit of salt. Heat a pan, coat it with oil and stir-fry.
- Cut the beef into thin strips, marinate and pan-fry.
- Wash the juice off the ripe *kimchi* cabbage and julienne.
- Boil the hand-cut noodles in clear beef broth, and season with Korean soy sauce (*guk-ganjang*) and salt.
- Transfer the noodles into a bowl, and garnish with julienned *aehobak*, beef and *kimchi*.

칼싹두기

SUMMER

녹두농마국수
Nokdu-nongma-guksu
Mung bean noodles with pine nut oil

Nongma is the North Korean word for starch powder. In Hwanghae-do Province, it is believed that a bowl of mung bean noodles could keep the doctor away. Mung beans, known for their cooling effect on the body, were especially popular in summer. *Nongma* noodles are typically served in broth, but at Onjium, they are made with mung bean powder and wheat flour, then tossed in pine nut oil and a generous amount of steamed mung bean crumbs to highlight the ingredient's flavour and aroma.

Ingredients

300 g (10½ oz) Korean whole wheat flour (bread flour made from *baekgangmil*, a type of Korean wheat)
60 g (2 oz) mung bean starch powder
160 ml (⅔ cup) water
1 tsp salt
90–100 g (½ cup) dehulled mung beans
135 g (4¾ oz) pine nuts (can be substituted for 3 tbsps pine nut oil or other nut oil such as walnut oil)
salt

Method
- Add mung bean starch powder and salt to the wheat flour, mix well, then add water and knead until somewhat stiff. Roll the mixture out thinly, then slice into ribbons to make the mung bean noodles.
- Soak the mung beans in water for about 5 hours and remove the remaining skin. Cook in a heated steamer and season lightly with salt while still hot.
- Toast the pine nuts in a pan and transfer them to an oil press to make pine nut oil, if making your own.
- Boil the mung bean noodles for about 2 minutes, rinse with cold water, then drain.
- Add salt and pine nut oil to the noodles and toss well. Mix in the steamed mung beans and serve.

SUMMER

민어어채
Mineo-eochae
Brown croaker fillet with vegetables

The royal court's stylish springtime recipe, *eochae*, has a long history. The royal kitchen preferred to serve lightly parboiled fish over raw fish. Tender, lean white fish fillets are seasoned with salt, drained, dusted with starch powder and briefly parboiled. Rinsing them in cold water immediately after cooking gives a smooth texture for easier swallowing. Mushrooms, cucumbers and red chillis are prepared in the same way and served together for visual appeal and balanced nutrition.

Ingredients
500 g (1 lb 1⅝) brown croaker fillet
3 shiitake mushrooms
2 farm-grown pine mushrooms (*cham-songyi-beoseot*)
1 Korean cucumber
1 green chilli
1 red chilli
30 g (1 oz) young radish greens
starch powder
vinegar *ganjang* (dipping sauce made with soy sauce and vinegar)
vinegar *gochujang* (dipping sauce made with Korean fermented chilli paste and vinegar)

Method
- Clean, gut, scale and debone the brown croaker. Fillet the meat and sprinkle some salt on it.
- Slice the shiitake mushrooms and tear the farm-grown pine mushrooms (*cham-songyi-beoseot*) into bite-sized shreds.
- Cut the cucumber lengthwise to deseed, then slice thinly into rectangular (*golpae*) shapes, roughly 3 cm (1¼ in.) by 2 cm (¾ in.).
- Slice the green and red chillis in half, deseed and cut them into rectangular shapes also.
- Pick out only tender, young leaves from the radish greens.
- Coat all prepared ingredients in starch powder, briefly parboil, then plunge into cold water and drain.
- Serve with vinegar *ganjang* and vinegar *gochujang* on the side.

SUMMER

수증계
Sujeung-gye
Chicken stuffed with mushroom filling

Onjium has reinterpreted a dish called *Sujeung-gye*, first introduced in *Eumsik-dimibang*, Korea's oldest cookbook. The original recipe describes roasting a chicken to a golden-brown, adding various vegetables, gently steaming it again, and garnishing with cucumber, chives and egg *jidan*. At Onjium, the chicken is stuffed with mushroom filling, boiled until tender, lightly pan-fried then topped with cucumber and chives, and served alongside warm mung bean porridge.

Ingredients
2 chickens
1 root of ginseng
90 g (½ cup) dehulled mung beans
90 g (½ cup) glutinous rice
dried kelp (*dasima*)
salt
black pepper powder
1 tbsp onion juice
1 tsp ginger juice

Stuffing
100 g (3½ oz) beef
beef marinade (*see *Okjamhwa-kkot-ssam*, page 148)
80 g (2¾ oz) onion
40 g (1½ oz) shiitake mushrooms
50 g (1¾ oz) sticky rice, cooked
starch powder

Garnish
1 Korean cucumber
50 g (1¾ oz) chives

Method
- Separate the chicken meat from the bones. Soak the bones in water to remove any blood, then boil with dried kelp (*dasima*). Strain the broth thoroughly.
- Thinly slice the thick part of the chicken breast and season with salt, pepper, onion juice and ginger juice.
- Soak the mung beans in water for dehulling. Wash them with water thoroughly.
- Add chunks of ginseng to the chicken broth and bring to a boil. Then, add the mung beans and cook until tender. Remove the ginseng and mung beans, then add the soaked sticky rice and bring to a boil. Once nearly cooked, grind in a food processor.

Making the stuffing
- Finely chop the beef and mix it with the beef marinade.
- Finely chop the onion, sprinkle a little salt on it, drain and stir-fry.
- Finely chop the shiitake mushrooms.
- Mix the cooked sticky rice and prepared ingredients together to make the stuffing.
- Cut the cucumber into 7 cm (2¾ in.) long slices, cut them into matchsticks and sprinkle with a little salt. Cut the chives into 7 cm (2¾ in.) long pieces. Lightly steam the cucumber and the chives in a bamboo steamer.
- Sprinkle starch powder on one side of the sliced chicken fillets, put the stuffing on it, roll it up, and cook in a preheated steamer.
- Lightly coat the surface with a starch powder batter and briefly pan-fry in an oil-coated pan before cutting into bite-sized pieces.
- Boil the ground broth made earlier and season with salt. Put the chicken in a bowl, pour over the broth, and garnish with the cucumber and chives.

SUMMER

맥적구이
Maegjeog-gui
Steamed pork belly seasoned and grilled with soybean paste

Steamed pork belly, seasoned with *doenjang* (fermented soybean paste) and grilled, offers a lighter flavour and softer texture. The *doenjang* and honey seasoning creates a simple yet rich taste.

Ingredients
1 kg (2 lb 4 oz) pork belly
1 spring onion (scallion)
1 onion
black peppercorns

Seasoning
2 tbsps *doenjang* (fermented soybean paste)
1 tbsp soy sauce
2 tbsps *mirin*
1 tbsp honey
1 tbsp chopped spring onion
1 tbsp crushed garlic
black pepper powder

Method
- Soak the pork belly in water for 3–4 hours to remove blood.
- Cut the spring onion (scallion) into 5 cm (2 in.) long slices and then cut them in half. Slice the onions into large pieces. Place the spring onion and the onion on top of the pork belly and cook them in a preheated steamer for 1½ hours.
- Combine all the seasoning ingredients to make the beef marinade.
- Cut the chilled meat into thick pieces and mix with the sauce.
- Coat a pan with oil and fry the pork.

SUMMER

호두잡채
Hodu-japchae
Walnuts with marinated beef and vegetables

Walnuts and pine nuts were introduced during the Goryeo dynasty, and in Gaeseong, walnuts were used in *japchae*, a dish in which various ingredients, cut into thin strips, are combined and mixed into a harmonious whole. Onjium's walnut *japchae* is made by serving marinated beef attached to walnuts so the two elements can be eaten together. Burdock (*ueong*) and chilli pepper add a crisp vegetable texture.

Ingredients
150 g (5¼ oz) whole walnuts
70 g (2½ oz) beef
beef marinade (*see *Okjamhwa-kkot-ssam*, page 148)
1 burdock root (*ueong*)
½ onion
2 green chilli peppers
1 red chilli pepper
starch powder
salt
sesame oil

Seasoning for the burdock (*ueong*)
160 ml (⅔ cup) water
1 tbsp soy sauce
salt
½ tbsp sugar
1 tbsp cooking oil
1 tbsp oligosaccharide syrup
½ tbsp perilla seed oil

Method
- Mince the beef and mix with the beef marinade.
- Dust the flat side of the walnuts with starch powder, then press on the marinated beef so the two elements are attached. Heat oil in a pan and cook meat-side down.
- Scrub the burdock root (*ueong*) clean and cut into 5 cm (2 in.) julienne strips. Cook in a pan with a little water until soft, then add soy sauce, salt, sugar and cooking oil. Simmer, then finish with oligosaccharide syrup and a drizzle of perilla seed oil.
- Cut the onion into julienne strips. Cut the chilli peppers in half, deseed and slice into julienne strips.
- Heat oil in a pan over a medium-high heat and stir-fry the onion. Add the peppers and season lightly with salt.
- Mix all ingredients well and add the sesame oil.

SUMMER

개성주악
Gaeseong Ju-ak
Deep fried rice cake coated with syrup

Ju-ak, also known as *umegi*, is a traditional dessert named for its cobblestone-like shape. It was made to celebrate the new rice harvest and, as the saying goes, 'There is no party without *umegi*' – it was a must at Gaeseong celebrations. The dough, made with *makgeolli* (a traditional Korean fermented rice alcoholic beverage), is kneaded, deep-fried and coated in *jipcheong* – spice-infused syrup – allowing it to stay soft for 2–3 days. *Ju-ak* is known for its flat shape with a wide central well and its distinctive flavour – sweet grain syrup infused with the scent of ginger.

Ingredients
420 g (3 cups) glutinous rice flour
5 tbsps wheat flour
3 tbsps sugar
5 tbsps *makgeolli* (a traditional Korean fermented rice alcoholic beverage)
1–1½ tbsps water, boiling
cooking oil

Jipcheong
240 ml (1 cup) *jocheong* (grain syrup)
120 ml (½ cup) of water
2 knobs of ginger, grated

Making Ju-ak
- Combine the glutinous rice flour and the wheat flour and pass the mixture through a sieve. Add sugar.
- Add the *makgeolli* (a traditional Korean fermented rice alcoholic beverage) to the sieved flour. Pour in the boiling water and knead for a long time.
- Shape the dough into flat rounds about 3 cm (1¼ in.) wide and 1 cm (⅜ in.) thick. Press the centre firmly to form a shallow well.
- Fry carefully at 180°C (350°F) until golden brown, making sure they don't stick together. Lower the oil to 150°C (300°F) and continue frying until cooked through.

Jipcheong
- Make the *jipcheong* by combining the *jocheong* (grain syrup), water and grated ginger in a pot. Bring to a boil and then turn off the heat.
- Soak the *ju-ak* in the syrup, then place on a sieve to drain the excess.

Essays on a Landscape: Gaeseong-bound

For nearly 500 years, Gaeseong stood as the capital of the Goryeo dynasty. Often referred to as Songak or Songdo – named after the rugged, pine-covered Songak Mountain – it remained the political and cultural heart of the kingdom until the capital was moved to Hanyang in 1396 during the Joseon dynasty. Over the centuries, the city was known by many names, including Gaegyeong, Junggyeong, Hwangdo and Wanggyeong. It would be no exaggeration to call Gaeseong the distilled essence of Goryeo – overflowing with the kingdom's vibrant, diverse and sophisticated culture.

Gaeseong was a flourishing metropolis, with records indicating a population of 100,000 households as early as the 13th century. The renowned Goryeo scholar Lee Gyubo praised the city's vitality and scale, writing: 'It is a thing of wonder. The tens of thousands of houses within the capital resemble a buzzing swarm of bees, while the countless people flowing through the main streets call to mind a drifting colony of ants.' He further described the commoners' quarters: 'The thousand gates and ten thousand homes are interlocked like the scales of a lesser dragon (*imugi*), aligned in neat rows like the teeth of a comb. The resulting sight is that of a dragon twisting and turning, and a phoenix in dance.'

Sadly, few landscape or folk paintings from the Goryeo period remain to offer a vivid depiction of Gaeseong's urban life and customs. As a result, we must turn to landscapes and maps created during the Joseon dynasty to catch a fleeting glimpse of old Gaeseong and immerse ourselves, however briefly, in its bygone atmosphere.

The 'Gijeondo' ('Map of Gyeonggi Province') section of the Donggugyeodo (Map of Korea)
19th century.
The Seoul National University Kyujanggak Institute for Korean Studies.

This colour copy of the *Donggugyeodo* (Map of Korea) is regarded as one of the most beautiful surviving old maps. Its painterly depiction of mountain ranges and rivers makes it a visual delight, showcasing a sophisticated and lush use of colour and linework. The *Donggugyeodo* marks not only cities and roads but also lookouts, temples and scenic spots, offering a rich visual representation of the landscape.

The *Gijeondo* maps out Gyeonggi Province, with particular significance in showing that Gaeseong was considered part of this region – an administrative classification that began in 1267 and persisted until the Korean War. Within the red circle in the upper left corner of the map lies Songdo (Gaeseong). Tracing westward along the waterway, one finds Byeokrando, the Goryeo kingdom's international trade port. East of Songdo are Jangdan and Paju, followed by Imjingak. Southward lies the capital (Hanyang, corresponding to the Joseon-era Seoul), with Samgak Mountain marking its northern boundary. Further down the peninsula appear Gwangju, Yongin, Suwon, Incheon, Yeongjong and Ganghwa – locations whose names and designations have endured to the present day.

Essays on a Landscape: Gaeseong-bound

The 'Songdo' section of the Haedongjido (Atlas of Korea)
18th century.
The Seoul National University Kyujanggak Institute for Korean Studies.

This map offers a meticulously detailed view of the many contours of Songdo, from the surrounding peaks and mountain ridges to the slender lines of rivers and streams that weave through the landscape. Scattered throughout are temples and hermitages, nestled in nearly every visible corner – a fitting reflection of historical records, which note that over 300 temples once stood in the Gaeseong area during the Goryeo period.

Let us begin at the centre of the map. Just above it lies the massive circular mountain fortress, formed by linking the lofty surrounding peaks – this is the Daeheung Mountain Fortress, guardian of the capital city and home to both Gwaneum Temple and Daeheung Temple. On the northern outskirts of the fortress, we find the famed Bagyeon Falls, where water cascades from a cliff of dark stone in a striking natural display.

Travelling diagonally downwards to the lower left-hand quarter of the map, we come upon Songak Mountain, and further south, the palace site of Manwoldae. Continuing past Gwandeokjeong and towards the right side of the fortress, we find Sungkyunkwan, followed by Seonjuk Bridge – historically significant as the site of Jeong Mongju's assassination. Tracing the path of the city ramparts, we also come to Namdaemun Gate. Gaeseong's fortress had a tripartite structure: Gungseong, the innermost enclosure, safeguarded the royal palace; Hwangseong served as the administrative heart, housing central government offices and the royal villa; and Naseong defined the city limits, fortifying the perimeter along the mountain ridges to defend against invasion.

The 'Songdo' section of the Haedongjido
(Atlas of Korea)

Songdogihaengcheop
(Album of a Journey to Songdo)
Kang Sehwang
32.8 × 53.4 cm (13 x 21 in.), ink and light colour on paper, c.1757.
The National Museum of Korea.

The Streets of Gaeseong
The first of the 16 paintings in the travel album offers a bird's eye view of Songak Mountain and of the Gaeseong streets with their orderly rows of roof-tiled houses (*giwajip*). The main road, beginning at the Nammullu Gate, is flanked by these houses on either side. It is rendered using Western-style perspective, causing the landscape to narrow and recede into the distance. This technique naturally guides the viewer's eye along the road, drawing it all the way towards Songak Mountain.

Daeheung Temple
Daeheung Temple was the largest of the many hermitages located within the mountain fortress that stretched between Cheonma Mountain and Seonggeo Mountain, north of Songdo. It housed a granary used to store provisions for military use. This depiction employs a single-point perspective to illustrate the temple's spatial layout – from the broad, trapezoidal courtyard to the ink-dark peak rising behind it. Rendered in meticulous detail are the vivid blue *dancheong* (traditional decorative colouring) of the Daeungjeon Hall, the multitiered brackets supporting the hip-and-gable roof, the slender supporting columns, the finely crafted latticework of the window grilles and the wooden latches affixed to the rafters.

A series of paintings by Kang Sehwang captures the landscapes of Songdo as they appeared in the mid-1700s. Kang Sehwang, a virtuous scholar (*seonbi*) of the late Joseon dynasty, was also an accomplished painter and art critic, and is well known as the mentor of artist Kim Hongdo. During this period, it became fashionable among men of letters to travel and paint from life, capturing notable landscapes encountered along the way. Following this trend, Kang Sehwang toured the Songdo region at the invitation of a prominent Gaeseong resident. The resulting travel album, *Songdogihaengcheop* (Album of a Journey to Songdo), features paintings of the 16 scenic sites he visited throughout the area.

The paintings in the *Songdogihaengcheop* primarily employ ink, yet they are distinguished by a limpid wash, subtle gradations in ink saturation and a carefully calibrated sense of depth that shifts with the proximity of depicted elements. Kang Sehwang skilfully applied perspective to create a realistic sense of distance, and each painting in the series demonstrates bold and innovative experimentation with the medium. In fact, Kang himself described the album in his epilogue as 'an album the likes of which the world has never seen'. By grounding his landscapes in direct observation rather than abstract idealization, Kang Sehwang ushered in a new chapter in late Joseon dynasty painting – introducing previously unexplored techniques of shading and perspective that set his work apart.

Yeongtongdong Entrance

As described in the epilogue, 'the stones set in disarray at the Yeongtongdong entrance are the size of houses and covered in green moss, so that the mere sight of them is enough to make the onlooker feel faint'. The painting presents a striking contrast between the towering moss-covered boulders and the solitary figure of a virtuous scholar (*seonbi*) making his way through them on a donkey. In a departure from convention, Kang Sehwang lays down a base of yellow and green, over which he applies Oriental ink to create depth and shading – an innovative technique that enhances the visual tension and texture of the scene.

Taejongdae

The painting depicts Taejongdae, a broad and flat rock on Seonggeo Mountain to the north of Gaeseong, set within a lush summer landscape teeming with dense greenery and a flowing stream. People are seen seeking relief from the heat, wading through the water with their trousers rolled up, while a lone figure – likely Kang Sehwang himself – paints on a sheet of paper spread across the expansive rock. The pale white water spray at the edge of the rock is rendered with delicate precision, reflecting the influence of Western painting techniques on Kang Sehwang's work.

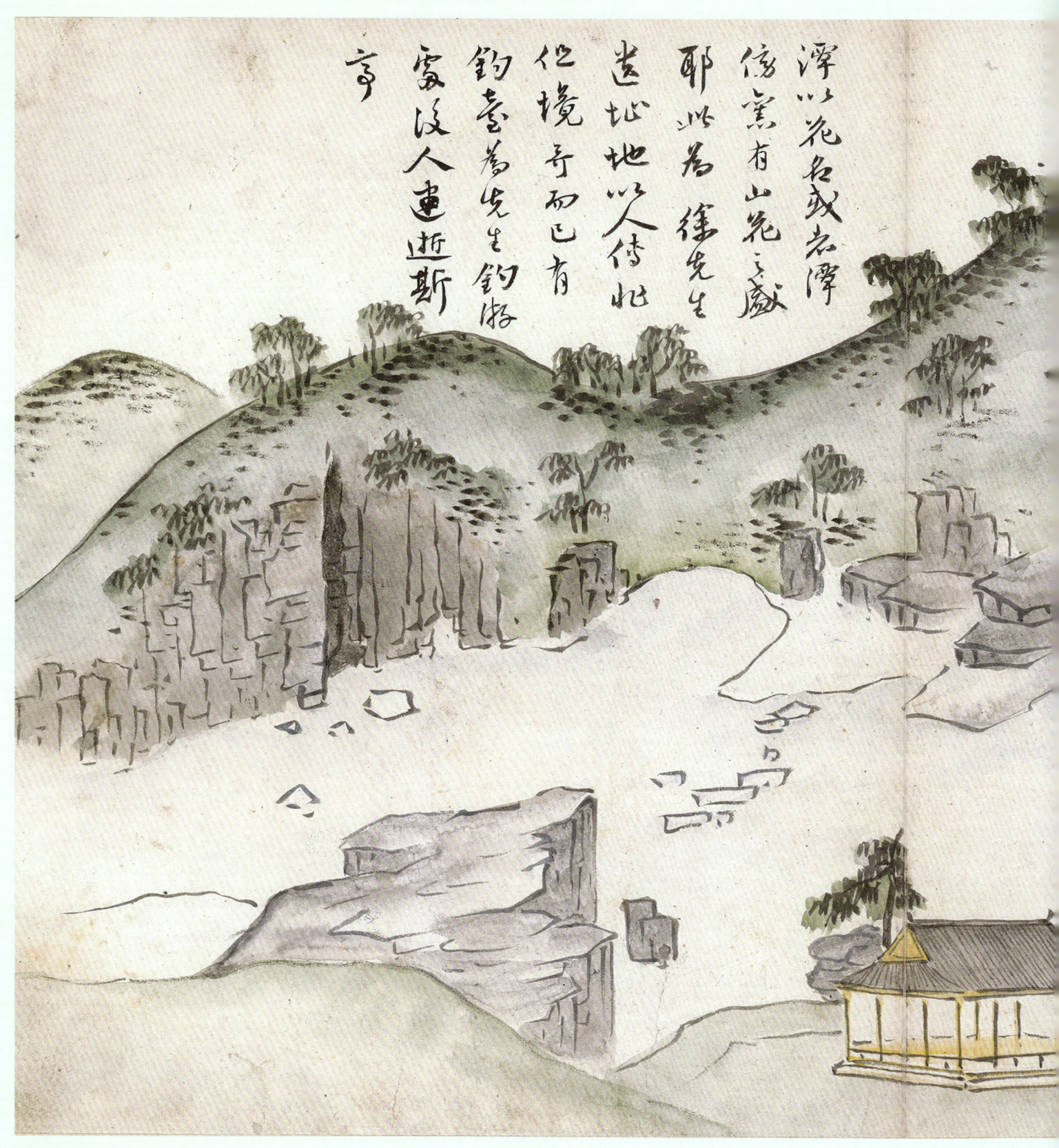

Songdogihaengcheop
(Album of a Journey to Songdo)
'Hwadam'
Kang Sehwang
32.8 × 53.4 cm (13 x 21 in.), ink and light colour on paper, c.1757.
The National Museum of Korea.

This painting captures the striking scenery of the Yeongtong Temple valley, nestled in Gaeseong's Ogwen Mountain, with the Hwadam Pavilion perched above, offering a commanding view of the surrounding landscape. The scene conveys both the tranquility of the valley and the majestic presence of the pavilion, blending nature's beauty with human architectural achievement.

Bagyeonpokpo (Bagyeon Falls)
Jeong Seon
119.7 × 52.2 cm (3 ft 11 × 1 ft 9 in.), ink and light colour on silk. Private Collection.

The Bagyeon Falls, located at the foot of Cheonma Mountain and Seonggeo Mountain, draw their appeal from the enthralling manner in which they pour with abandon from between black rock that rises into the air like a colossal embankment. In stark contrast to Kang Sehwang and his lifelike landscapes, Jeong Seon chooses to fully exaggerate the scale of the falls through the robust and bracing effect of an elongated and narrow configuration. The painting accordingly makes it seem as though the instant rush of water and its straightforward and resounding crash have descended on our eardrums. The magnitude of the downpour is all the more overpowering, emphasized by the minuscule figure painted below the falls.

A long-running stream of heaven erupts from the edge of the rocks
A hundred lengths of falling water rush on without end
The swooping torrent surges up and descends like a galaxy
And the enraged waterfall hung aslant reveals a white rainbow
    for all to see
Potent droplets fill the valley in a daze
Shattered beads and jade pierce the clear skies
Do not say, oh wayfarer, that Yeosan is preferable
For Cheonma Mountain is by rights peerless in our land

From the roar of cascading water to the sparkling mist diffusing far away into the air, famed Gaeseong courtesan (*gisaeng*) and writer Hwang Jini's traditional poem (*sijo*) paints a portrait of the Bagyeon Falls and its majestic spectacle in sharp relief.

**Giroseryeongyedo
(The Fraternal Legacy of Elders)**
Kim Hongdo
147.2 × 63.3 cm (4 ft 10 × 2 ft 1 in.), ink and
light colour on silk. Private Collection.

Kim Hongdo's *Giroseryeongyedo* (The Fraternal Legacy of Elders) is a genre painting (*pungsokdo*) depicting a feast in honor of the elderly held within the old palace site of Manwoldae at the southern foothold of the Songak Mountain in Gaeseong. The term *giro* refers to elders over the age of sixty, while *seryeongye* denotes feasts held by the kingdom in the spring and fall seasons. Having amassed considerable wealth through the ginseng trade, the merchants of Gaeseong are said to have commissioned a piece of art from court painter Kim Hongdo in commemoration of this particular feast. A list of the 64 elders honoured at the feast can be found at the bottom of the painting.

Beneath the peak of Songak Mountain stippled with autumn light lies a pine forest wrapped in mist; over the stonework of Manwoldae hangs a large awning. In the shade of the awning are 64 white-bearded old men seated one after another in front of a folding screen as they receive their own tables. Contrary to the uniform postures of the guests, the dancing children, musicians, cooks, horsemen and onlookers outside the awning are characterized by their liveliness and distinctive range.

Manwoldae was initially the site of a monumental palace built by King Taejo to mark the dawn of the Goryeo dynasty, but due to foreign invasion, rebellion and fire damage, the palace itself became a remnant of the past, leaving only a stony foundation in its wake.

An erstwhile thing of glory reduced to its desolate vestiges, Manwoldae appears in the traditional poems (*sijo*) of the late Goryeo and early Joseon periods as a scene of devastation overgrown with fading grasses and is accordingly symbolic of the futility and transience of old splendours. One example of such usage is Won Cheonseok's 'Song of Retrospection', which speaks of a heart steeped in grief upon seeing Manwoldae overrun with weeds and looking back on the bygone magnificence of Goryeo's 500-year history.

The vicissitudes of fortune being given their time and place,
 even Manwoldae is now autumn grass
Five hundred years of a dynasty fill the sound of a shepherd's flute
And bring tears to a wayfarer passing by at sundown

가을

AUTUMN

bringing splendour of fruition

AUTUMN

밤죽
Bam-juk
Chestnut porridge

Finely ground, well-ripened chestnuts gathered in autumn are added to rice porridge. Their sweet, rich flavor makes the dish especially tempting, though overboiling can diminish the distinctive taste of the chestnuts.

Ingredients
300 g (10½ oz) chestnuts
480 ml (2 cups) water
60 g (⅓ cup) rice
480 ml (2 cups) milk
salt

Method
- Slice the chestnuts crosswise into pieces. Boil in water for 20 minutes. Drain and grind finely.
- Soak rice in water for 1 hour and drain. Add a little water and grind finely.
- Put the ground chestnuts and rice in a large pot. Add 480 ml (2 cups) of water and boil for 20 minutes. Turn the heat to low. Add milk and bring to a boil at a low heat. Season with salt.

밤죽

AUTUMN

송이전복탕
Songyi-jeonbok-tang
Pine mushrooms and abalone soup

Pine mushrooms are the most prized of all autumn mushrooms, cherished for their intense aroma and distinctive flavour. When abalones are slow-cooked for over an hour and pine mushrooms are added to the warm stock, the result is a refined and deeply flavourful seasonal soup – an exquisite appetizer for autumn.

Ingredients
5 abalones
1 stalk of spring onion (scallion), cut into 5 pieces
4 pine mushrooms
1 *seogi* mushroom
720 ml (3 cups) of beef brisket broth (*see page 90)
chopped spring onion
crushed garlic
3 tbsps *cheongju* (Korean rice wine)
salt

Method
- Place the abalones shell-side down in a basket set over boiling water. Drizzle the *cheongju* (Korean rice wine) over the abalones. Top with the spring onion (scallion) and steam for 1½ hours. Remove the abalone meat from the shells. Cut diagonally into 3 or 4 pieces.
- Wipe the pine mushrooms clean with a damp cloth, then tear them into thin strips by hand. Soak the *seogi* mushrooms in water for about 20 minutes, then drain and shred them into thin strips.
- Place the chopped spring onion and crushed garlic in a fine mesh strainer and steep them in the boiled beef brisket broth. Season the broth with salt.
- Place the abalone in a bowl and ladle in the beef brisket broth. Top with pine mushroom strips and garnish with shredded *seogi* mushroom.

송이전복탕
Songyi-jeonbok-tang

게살배추선
Gesal-baechu-seon
Steamed napa cabage stuffed with snow crab meat

Napa cabbage reaches its peak in autumn and Koreans have long enjoyed using it in stuffed and steamed vegetable dishes during this season. Known for its natural sweetness and mild flavour, napa cabbage is ideal for steaming. This dish is made by layering a savoury filling between the leaves. While beef is the traditional choice, using crab meat instead elevates the dish into something truly special.

Ingredients

200 g (7 oz) yellowish heart of a napa cabbage
1 snow crab
3 fresh shiitake mushrooms, shredded
70 g (2½ oz) oyster mushrooms (*neutari-beoseot*),
 torn thinly by hand
1 courgette (zucchini), cut into matchsticks 3 cm (1¼ in.) long
100 g (3½ oz) mung bean sprouts, heads and tails removed
720 ml (3 cups) *dasima myeolchi* stock (*see page 22)
Korean soy sauce (*guk-ganjang*)
Korean water celery or *minari* (Korean watercress)
salt
pepper

Method

- Clean the yellowish heart of the napa cabbage.
- Steam the crab for 15 minutes over boiling water. Remove the meat.
- Season both types of mushrooms with salt and pepper, then stir-fry. Lightly salt the courgette (zucchini) and stir-fry until just tender. Blanch the mung bean sprouts and *minari* (Korean watercress) in boiling water, then drain well. Combine the mushrooms, courgette and mung bean sprouts, and season with salt to taste.
- Mix the seasoned vegetables with crab meat and carefully stuff the mixture into the leaves of the napa cabbage. Secure each roll by tying the ends with *minari* stalks.
- Boil the *dasima myeolchi* stock in a pot. Season with Korean soy sauce (*guk-ganjang*) and salt.
- Place the stuffed napa cabbage in the pot and boil for 10 minutes, occasionally pouring the stock over the cabbage to ensure it cooks evenly and absorbs the flavours.

AUTUMN

전어무침
Jeoneo-muchim
Jeoneo with vegetables

Jasaneobo, a record of fish from the waters off Heuksan-do Island written by Jeong Yak-jeon in 1814, describes *jeoneo* (gizzard shad) as a fatty, sweet fish. It reaches its peak in fat content in autumn, especially in October, when it is considered most delicious. While *Jeoneo* is typically grilled, a seasonal delicacy is raw *jeoneo* served with *sangchu* (Korean lettuce) tossed in *doenjang* (fermented soybean paste) seasoned with Sichuan pepper.

Ingredients
4–5 *jeoneo*, descaled, with head and innards removed
70 g (2½ oz) *sangchu* (Korean lettuce)
7 perilla leaves
½ onion, shredded
2 green peppers, cut in half and then finely shredded
½ red pepper, cut in half and then finely shredded
100 g (3½ oz) white radish, cut into thin matchsticks 5 cm (2 in.) long
salt

Seasoning for the doenjang (fermented soybean paste)
doenjang (fermented soybean paste)
gochujang
vinegar
plum extract
oligosaccharide
apple juice
Sichuan pepper

Method
- Slice the *jeoneo* and rinse in cold salted water. Pat dry with a paper towel. Cut diagonally into thin strips.
- Tear the *sangchu* (Korean lettuce) and perilla leaves by hand. Rinse the onion in cold water.
- Make *doenjang* (fermented soybean paste) seasoning by mixing all the relevant ingredients together.
- Season the fish strips with sesame oil and salt just before serving. Toss the vegetables with the *doenjang* seasoning. Arrange the fish and vegetables on a plate for serving.

AUTUMN

먹버섯 갈비찜구이
Meok-beoseot galbi-jjim-gui
Grilled steamed beef short ribs with meok mushroom

This beef rib dish is more mildly seasoned than ordinary braised ribs and has been handed down for generations by the Heo family clan in Jisu-myeon, Gyeongsangnam-do. A braised beef short rib dish was traditionally served at holiday dinners, on the ancestral ritual table, or to treat guests. Onjium has added chewy *meok* mushrooms, a type of edible wild mushroom harvested only in autumn and known for its dark colour and rich flavour. The beef ribs become more savoury and tender if steamed before being grilled.

Ingredients
600 g (1 lb 5⅛ oz) beef ribs
50 g (1¾ oz) *meok* mushrooms
150 g (5¼ oz) chopped onion
2 chestnuts, skinned and chopped
70 g (2½ oz) Korean pear, chopped
2 Korean dates (*jujubes*), cut in thin strips
starch

Beef seasoning
2 tbsps soy sauce
1 tbsp sugar
½ tbsp honey
2 tbsps chopped spring onion (scallion)
1 tbsp crushed garlic
4 tbsps flour
salt

Method
- Cut the ribs into 10 cm (4 in.) long pieces. Trim the excess fat from the ribs. Carefully remove the meat from the bones and mince it coarsely. Set aside the rib bones for later use.
- Stir-fry the onion. Parboil the *meok* mushrooms. Cut into thin strips. Mix the minced meat with the mushrooms, onion, chestnut and pear.
- Sprinkle starch over the bones. Top the bones with the meat mixture and steam over boiling water for 15 minutes.
- Place the steamed meat and rib bones on the grate and grill the surface until lightly charred. Once grilled, transfer to a plate and top with the Korean-date (*jujube*) strips.

AUTUMN

능이 송이버섯밥
Neungi-songyi-beoseot-bap
Rice with autumn mushrooms

With the cool autumn breeze comes the season to enjoy the delicate flavours of mushrooms. Chewy mushrooms harvested in autumn are rich in flavour. Rice cooked with a variety of mushrooms – pine mushrooms with their hint of woody aroma, shingled hedgehog mushrooms (*neungi-beoseot*) with their unique flavour and scent, shiitake mushrooms, and golden enoki mushrooms (*hwanggeum paengi-beoseot*) – becomes a very special seasonal dish, rich in nutrients.

Ingredients
360 g (2 cups) rice
50 g (1¾ oz) shingled hedgehog mushrooms (*neungi-beoseot*), cut into bite-sized pieces
60 g (2 oz) oyster mushrooms (*neutari-beoseot*), cut into bite-sized pieces
60 g (2 oz) golden enoki mushrooms (*hwanggeum paengi-beoseot*), cut into bite-sized pieces
50 g (1¾ oz) lion's mane mushrooms (*norugungdengi-beoseot*), cut into bite-sized pieces
2 fresh shiitake mushrooms, shredded
salt
sesame oil

Seasoning for the shingled hedgehog mushrooms (*neungi-beoseot*)
½ tsp Korean soy sauce (*guk-ganjang*)
½ tsp chopped spring onion (scallion)
⅓ tsp minced garlic
1 tsp perilla seed oil

Seasoned soy sauce
1 tbsp soy sauce
1 tbsp Korean soy sauce
2 tbsps *dasima myeolchi* stock (*see page 22)
1 tsp sugar
1 tbsp chopped spring onion
1 tsp crushed garlic
1 tbsp sesame oil

Method
- Soak rice in water for 30 minutes.
- Parboil the shingled hedgehog mushrooms (*neungi-beoseot*), then strain and set aside the water used for parboiling. Gently wipe the dirt from the pine mushrooms using a damp cloth and cut them lengthwise into quarters. Season the oyster mushrooms (*neutari-beoseot*), golden enoki mushrooms (*hwanggeum paengi-beoseot*) and lion's mane mushrooms (*norugungdengi-beoseot*) with salt and sesame oil, then stir-fry. Toss the shingled hedgehog mushrooms with seasoning and stir-fry separately.
- Put the ice in a pan and top with the shingled hedgehog mushrooms. Pour in 480 ml (2 cups) of the water used to parboil the mushrooms set aside earlier and bring to a boil. Reduce the heat to low, add the remaining mushrooms, and simmer gently for about 10 minutes.
- Scoop the cooked rice into bowls. Arrange the mushrooms on top and serve with seasoned soy sauce on the side.

AUTUMN

백화반
Baek-hwaban
Bibimbap with white vegetables

Typical *bibimbap* is known for its vibrant variety of vegetables, each contributing a different colour. It is often called *hwaban*, meaning 'flower plate', for the harmonious beauty created by the colours of the vegetables topping the rice. Onjium has reimagined this dish by using only white-coloured vegetables, naming it *baek-hwaban*, or 'white flower plate', to reflect its refined monochrome elegance.

Ingredients
360 g (2 cups) rice, rinsed, soaked in water for 30 minutes and then cooked
100 g (3 ½ oz) *doraji* (bellflower root) peeled and cut into thin matchsticks 5 cm (2 in.) long
100 g (3 ½ oz) *deodeok* (lance asiabell roots), peeled and cut into thin matchsticks 5 cm (2 in.) long
200 g (7 oz) white gourd (*dongah*), peeled and cut into thin matchsticks 5 cm (2 in.) long
150 g (5¼ oz) white radish, peeled and cut into thin matchsticks 5 cm (2 in.) long
50 g (1¾ oz) *cheongpo-muk* (mung bean jelly), shredded
2 chestnuts, inner skin peeled and then finely shredded

Seasoning for the vegetables
chopped spring onion (scallion)
crushed garlic
ginger juice
sesame oil
salt

Method
- Rub the *doraji* (bellflower root) in salted water to remove any bitterness.
- Add oil to a preheated frying pan. Stir-fry all the prepared vegetables, adding vegetable seasoning to taste.
- Blanch the shredded *cheongpo-muk* (mung bean jelly) in boiling water and strain. Season with salt and sesame oil.
- Scoop rice into a bowl. Top with the stir-fried vegetables and *cheongpo-muk*. Garnish with the shredded chestnuts.

AUTUMN

연근전
Yeongeun-jeon
Lotus root pancake

Lotus root is valued not only as a culinary ingredient but also as a medicinal herb. One way to enjoy its crisp texture is to slice it crosswise into thick rounds and pan-fry in oil. Alternatively, lotus root can be grated and mixed with flour to form a batter for pancakes. Dropping small spoonfuls of the batter into a hot pan and flattening them into thin rounds yields pancakes that are crispy on the outside and tender inside. For added flavour, prawns (shrimp) can be mixed into the batter, making the lotus root pancakes even more delicious.

Ingredients
2 medium-size lotus roots, peeled
120 ml (½ cup) *dasima myeolchi* stock (*see page 22)
50 g (⅓ cup) soft flour
50 g (⅓ cup) medium flour
Korean soy sauce (*guk-ganjang*)
sesame oil

Method
- Grate 1 lotus root and shred the other lotus root.
- Add flour, Korean soy sauce (*guk-ganjang*) and sesame oil to *dasima myeolchi* stock and stir well.
- Pour the flour mixture over the lotus root and mix well. Drop spoonfuls of the batter mixture into a hot pan to form bite-sized rounds and flatten gently. Cook until both sides are golden brown and crisp.

AUTUMN

깨강정
Kkae-gangjeong
Sesame crunch

To use white sesame seeds as garnish, they must first be skinned and then roasted. This sesame crunch is made from white sesame seeds that have undergone that meticulous process. While making this sesame crunch is undoubtedly time-consuming, the result is well worth the time and effort. Unlike the typical evenly cut rectangular sesame crunch, Onjium rolls it out with a rolling pin into a thin, paper-like crisp – resembling delicate potato chips.

Ingredients
60 g (2 oz) white seeds, soaked in water for 12 hours and then peeled
1 tbsp sugar
1⅓ tbsps oligosaccharide syrup
1 tsp water
salt

Method
- Roast the sesame seeds on a dry frying pan then remove.
- Add the sugar, oligosaccharide, water and salt to the pan. Let it bubble up. Reduce to a low heat.
- Add the sesame seeds. Stir well until the seeds are evenly coated with the syrup.
- Place a small ball of the mixture on a cutting board and roll it out with a rolling pin into a thin, crisp-like shape. Let the crisps rest until firm.

깨강정
Kkae-gangjeong

AUTUMN

육포다식
Yukpo-dasik
Pressed cookie made of beef jerky

Honey should be added to the seasoning for beef jerky to keep it tender; without it, the jerky can become tough and dry. This slightly sweet and salty beef jerky pairs well with pine nuts. A special treat called *dasik* – a pressed Korean cookie – is made by combining shredded beef jerky with finely minced pine nuts, resulting in a delicately layered snack with a rich, savoury flavour.

Beef jerky

500 g (1 lb 1⅝ oz) beef, outside round or bottom round
3½ tbsps soy sauce
⅔ tbsp honey
1 tbsp sugar
2 tbsps Korean pear juice
1 knob of fresh ginger
1 dried red pepper

Method

- Slice beef 6–7 mm (¼ in.) thick. Remove blood by patting with a paper towel. Set aside.
- Add all ingredients to the soy sauce except the honey. Boil for about 5 minutes on a low heat. Strain through a sieve. Add the honey to the stock. Let it cool.
- Marinate the beef in the cooled soy sauce stock. Let the soy sauce absorb completely into the beef.
- Dry the beef in a shaded place with good air ventilation: spread the beef flat on a wicker tray. Dry for 3 hours. Turn and dry the other side.

Dasik (pressed cookie)

60 g (2 oz) beef jerky
2 tsps oligosaccharide syrup
1 tsp roasted sesame seeds
5 tbsps ground pine nuts

Method

- Cut the beef jerky into small pieces. Stir-fry in a pan or grill on a grate.
- Finely grind the beef jerky and sesame seeds separately. Add the sesame seeds and oligosaccharide syrup to the beef and mix together well, then knead.
- Put ground pine nuts in a *dasik*-pan (*dasik* mould), then add the beef jerky mixture on top. Press firmly to impress the pattern.

AUTUMN

속미음
Sok-mieum
Dates and ginseng porridge

Juk is made by soaking grains in water, then grinding and simmering them. *Mieum*, on the other hand, simmers whole grains until they soften and is sifted. *Mieum* is typically thinner than *juk*, resembling more of a gruel. To make *sok-mieum*, glutinous rice, Korean dates (*jujubes*) and fresh ginseng are simmered together on a low heat. *Sok-mieum* is known for soothing and warming both the stomach and the soul.

Ingredients
500 g (1 lb 1⅝ oz) dried Korean dates (*jujubes*)
2.5 L (2½ qts) water
180 g (1 cup) glutinous rice, soaked in water
2 fresh Korean ginseng roots (*insam*)
salt

Method
- Wash the Korean dates (*jujubes*), score them, put in a pan of water and boil for about 1 hour. When the dates soften, strain the juice through a sieve.
- Transfer the date juice and soaked rice into a pan and simmer.
- Wash the fresh Korean ginseng roots (*insam*) thoroughly, slice them into thin rounds, and give them a quick rinse with water.
- Once the mixture reaches a soupy consistency, turn off the heat and let it rest for a few minutes. Season with salt, then ladle into bowls and garnish with the sliced ginseng.

속미음

AUTUMN

옥잠화 꽃쌈
Okjamhwa-kkot-ssam
Marinated beef wrapped with August-lilies

August-lilies, which bloom across Korea in summer, produce pure white flowers whose slender buds resemble traditional white jade hairpins, or *binyeo*. This likeness gave rise to the flower's poetic name, *okjamhwa*, meaning 'jade *binyeo* flower' in Chinese characters. Onjium celebrates the end of summertime with this fragrant, bite-sized dish: August-lily flower buds delicately stuffed with stir-fried beef and mushrooms, and topped with thin strips of Korean pear. The dish reflects the heart of traditional Korean culture – finding and savouring beauty in every part of nature, even amid the heat of summer, and bringing that appreciation to the table.

Ingredients
5 August-lily flower buds
100 g (3½ oz) lean beef cut
2 shiitake mushrooms
⅙ Korean pear
3 bunches of spring onions (scallions)
salt
sesame oil

Beef marinade (per 100g (3½ oz) of beef)
1 tsp Korean soy sauce (*guk-ganjang*)
1 tbsp soy sauce
1 tsp sugar
1 tbsp minced spring onion
½ tbsp crushed garlic
1 tsp sesame oil
black pepper

Method
- Remove the stamens from the August-lilies, rinse quickly under water, and gently pat dry.
- Slice the beef into julienne strips and massage in the marinade. Stir-fry over medium heat until the moisture evaporates.
- Cut the shiitake mushrooms into julienne strips, then dry-roast in a pan. Lightly season with salt and finish with a drizzle of sesame oil before turning off the heat.
- Julienne the pear into 3 cm (1¼ in.) long strips.
- Toss the stir-fried beef and shiitake mushrooms together, then mix in the chopped spring onions (scallions).
- Stuff the mixture into the August-lily flower buds and top with Korean pear strips. Arrange neatly on a plate to serve.

옥잠화 꽃쌈
Okjamhwa-kkot-ssam

AUTUMN

모둠회
Modum-hwe
Assorted raw and pickled fish

Modum-hwe is a beautifully arranged assortment of seasonal seafood. Onjium's version features lightly pickled amberjack and Pacific herring for a refreshing bite, sweet and spicy northern prawns (shrimp), blanched and peeled octopus, and *mugeunji* (aged *kimchi*) that ties all the flavours together. The rich Pacific herring is simply seasoned with salt and oil, paired with a crisp cucumber salad, while the fresh northern prawns are served with a soy sauce-based dressing made from dried kelp (*dasima*), Korean chestnuts, Korean dates (*jujubes*) and thinly sliced garlic strips.

Bangeo-hwe (lightly pickled amberjack)
300 g (10½ oz) fresh, raw amberjack
salt

Method
- Trim the amberjack by removing the spines and skin, then slice it thickly and season with salt.

Cheongeo-hwe (lightly pickled Pacific herring and cucumber salad)
2 fresh, raw Pacific herrings
1 Korean cucumber
⅓ onion
salt
sesame oil

Method
- Fillet the Pacific herrings, cut into strips and season with salt and sesame oil.
- Cut the cucumber in half lengthwise, then slice it diagonally. Sprinkle with salt and let it pickle for about 10 minutes. Squeeze out the moisture and massage with sesame oil.
- Julienne the onion, and toss together with the Pacific herring and cucumber.

Recipe continues on next page

Dansaeu-mu-jeot (seasoned raw northern prawns)
200 g (7 oz) fresh, raw northern prawns (shrimp)
3 tbsps seasoned soy sauce
50 g (1¾ oz) Korean chestnuts
30 g (1 oz) dried Korean dates (*jujubes*)
30 g (1 oz) garlic
15 g (½ oz) ginger
15 g (½ oz) spring onion (scallion)
generous amount of toasted sesame seeds

Seasoned soy sauce for dressing
240 ml (1 cup) soy sauce
240 ml (1 cup) water
60 ml (¼ cup) sake
dried kelp (*dasima*)
1 tbsp sugar
1 tbsp oligosaccharide syrup
5 tbsps coarse Korean chilli powder
2 tbsps fine Korean chilli powder

Method
- Peel the prawns (shrimp) and rinse them in lightly salted water, then drain.
- To make the dressing, combine soy sauce, water, dried kelp (*dasima*) and sake in a saucepan and bring to a boil. Turn off the heat and let it cool. Once cooled, add oligosaccharide syrup and Korean chilli powder.
- Julienne the chestnuts, dates, garlic and ginger, chop the spring onion (scallion) and put everything into the sauce.
- Pour the sauce over the prepared northern prawns.

Mugeunji
½ head of *mugeunji* (aged *kimchi*)

Mugeunji dressing
2½ tbsps soy sauce
2 tbsps Korean plum extract
2 tbsps *mirin*
2 tbsps water
1 tsp sesame oil

Method
- Rinse the *mugeunji* (aged *kimchi*), then drain well. Roughly chop into 4 cm (1½ in.) lengths. Mix the dressing ingredients together, then soak the ripened *kimchi* in the dressing. Remove the *kimchi* from the dressing before serving.

Blanched octopus
⅓ leg of raw giant Pacific octopus
⅓ Korean radish
1 tbsp dried green tea leaves
Korean soy sauce (*guk-ganjang*)

Method
- Rinse the octopus leg multiple times to remove the slime.
- Grate the Korean radish and let the octopus soak in it for about 30 minutes.
- Put green tea leaves in boiling water, season with Korean soy sauce (*guk-ganjang*), and cook the octopus in it. Boil for 9 to 14 minutes, depending on the size, then chill. Remove the skin and slice thinly.

AUTUMN

천렵국
Cheollyeop-guk
River fish spicy soup

Cheollyeop literally means 'river fishing'. *Cheollyeop-guk* is a traditional soup made with freshly caught freshwater fish, typically enjoyed on a summer day by a stream. The Gaeseong-style version is a distinctive spicy soup that includes not only fish such as golden mandarin fish and amur catfish, but also beef and a variety of greens. Young summer radish is often preferred over *ugeoji* (the tough, outer leaves) for this dish. After enjoying the main ingredients, the remaining broth is commonly reused as a base for *sujebi* (hand-pulled buckwheat noodles) or a nourishing fish porridge. This recipe yields 5–6 servings.

Ingredients
1 kg (2 lb 4 oz) golden mandarin fish
1 kg (2 lb 4 oz) amur catfish
1 kg (2 lb 4 oz) smaller catch (any fresh-water fish)
dried kelp (*dasima*)
720 ml (3 cups) beef broth
400 g (14 oz) water celery
400 g (14 oz) chives
400 g (14 oz) young radish
200 g (7 oz) spring onion (scallion)
5 chilli peppers
Korean soy sauce (*guk-ganjang*)
2 tbsps *gochujang*
2 tbsps Korean chilli powder
1 tbsp *doenjang* (fermented soybean paste)
1 tbsp crushed garlic

Method
- Clean, scale and gut the golden mandarin fish and amur catfish. Pan-fry any smaller catch in a pan until the moisture disappears, then season with Korean soy sauce (*guk-ganjang*). Add water and dried kelp (*dasima*), bring to a boil, and simmer for about 30 minutes. Strain through a sieve.
- Mix the fish broth with beef broth, then add *gochujang*, Korean chilli powder and *doenjang* (fermented soybean paste). Simmer gently.
- Wash the vegetables and cut them into 5 cm (2 in.) long pieces.
- Once the flavours have melded, add the golden mandarin fish, amur catfish and vegetables. Bring to a boil. Add crushed garlic as a final touch.
- Enjoy the soup, and use the leftover broth to make *sujebi* (hand-pulled buckwheat noodles) using buckwheat dough.

AUTUMN

해삼찜
Haesam-jjim
Steamed sea cucumber roll with prawns

A dish where the interior of a carefully soaked sea cucumber is filled with tender ingredients and then steamed. While meat is a common filling, Onjium's variation features prawns (shrimp) for a lighter, more refined flavour.

Ingredients
3 dried sea cucumbers, soaked in water
100 g (3½ oz) prawns (shrimp)
30 g (1 oz) tofu
1 tbsp flour
2 eggs
1 tbsp starch powder
100 ml (½ cup) beef broth
salt
Korean soy sauce (*guk-ganjang*)

Prawn (shrimp) sauce
salt
2 tsps minced spring onion (scallion)
1 tsp crushed garlic
½ tsp ginger juice
1 tsp sesame oil

Method
- Finely chop the prawns (shrimp) and mix with the prawn sauce.
- Drain the tofu, crush it, season with salt and sesame oil, and mix with the prawns.
- Lightly dust the inside of the sea cucumber with flour and stuff it with the filling.
- Separate the egg whites from the yolks, season each with a pinch of salt and beat well.
- Sprinkle starch over the stuffed sea cucumber. Steam in a bamboo steamer for about 5 minutes, taking care to preserve the original shape. Slice the sea cucumber and serve, or coat with the beaten egg and pan-fry.
- Season the clear beef broth with salt and Korean soy sauce (*guk-ganjang*).
- Put the steamed sea cucumber in a bowl and ladle over the broth.

AUTUMN

게구이
Ge-gui
Soft crab meat pancake

Soft crab meat is mixed with egg and gently steamed. The steamed mixture is then cut, skewered with spring onion (scallion) and pan-fried in a glutinous rice flour batter. As this dish requires considerable effort, discerning diners are sure to appreciate every bite of its delicate crab flavour.

Ingredients
1 kg (2 lb 4 oz) fresh blue crab
70 g (2½ oz) spring onion (scallion)
4 eggs
10 g (⅓ oz) starch powder
1 tsp ginger juice
black pepper powder
150 g (1 cup) glutinous rice flour
skewers

Method
- Deshell the fresh blue crabs by opening the shell from the back. Remove the gills and cut the crabs in half. Carefully extract the roe and gently press to obtain the lump meat.
- Mix the crab meat and innards, then add egg, starch powder, ginger juice and black pepper to make crab mixture. Spread it evenly in a mould about 1 cm (⅜ in.) high and steam in a steamer.
- Trim the spring onion (scallion), steam for about 1 minute, and roll into 5 cm (2 in.) long ties.
- Slice the steamed crab mixture to match the size of the spring onion and skewer them alternately.
- Coat in glutinous rice flour batter and pan-fry in a lightly oiled pan.

게구이

AUTUMN

순대구이
Soondae-gui
Grilled pork sausage

Pigs fed exclusively on rice hulls produce lean meat with minimal fat and a light, clean flavour. Gaeseong-style *soondae*, known as *jeolchang* (which literally means 'the best intestines'), is made by stuffing the intestines of these pigs with a mixture of pork blood, glutinous rice, mung bean sprouts, chives and tofu. The savory, tender slices of *soondae* are typically enjoyed freshly boiled and cut on the spot, but they're also delicious when quickly pan-fried in oil. In Gaeseong, *soondae* was traditionally eaten with pork, so they are shown in the image opposite side by side. This recipe yields 8–10 servings.

Ingredients
500 g (1 lb 1⅝ oz) pork intestines

Soondae stuffing
1.5 kg (3 lb 5 oz) pork
1 spring onion (scallion)
400 g (14 oz) beef
1 kg (2 lb 4 oz) *seonji* (blood clot)*
300 g (10½ oz) sticky rice, cooked
800 g (1 lb 12 oz) cabbage
200 g (7 oz) chives
300 g (10½ oz) onions
100 g (3½ oz) shiitake mushrooms
50 g (1¾ oz) green chilli peppers
50 g (1¾ oz) red chilli peppers
20 g (¾ oz) perilla leaves
80g (2¾ oz) chopped spring onion
60 g (2 oz) crushed garlic
salt

Preparing the pork intestines
- Sprinkle flour over the pork intestines and gently massage to clean. Turn them inside out and repeat the process with more flour to thoroughly wash.

Preparing the stuffing
- Drain the blood from the pork. Place the spring onion (scallion) and the pork in a steamer and cook for 1½ hours, then let cool. Grind in a food processor.
- Drain the blood from the beef, boil it, then grind in a food processor.
- Place the blood clot in sieve to drain excess blood.
- Cut the cabbage into quarters, steam and slice the chives thinly.
- Finely chop the onion and mince the shiitake mushrooms.
- Cut the chilli peppers in half, remove the seeds and chop. Cut the perilla leaves into thin slices.
- Mix the prepared pork, beef, blood clot, sticky rice and vegetables. Add the spring onion and garlic, season with salt, and mix thoroughly.

Method
- Insert a funnel into the pork intestines and carefully fill with the prepared stuffing.
- Form sausages (*soondae*) about 40–50 cm (16–20 in.) long, leaving about 10 cm (4 in.) unfilled at each end. Tie both ends securely with cotton thread.
- Bring a large pot of water to a rolling boil. Briefly blanch the *soondae*, then transfer to a steamer. Steam for about 20 minutes. Let cool slightly, then cut into bite-sized slices to serve.
- Heat oil in a pan and fry both sides until golden brown.

* *Soondae* is similar to boudin or sausage. It is typically made with beef or pork blood, but when blood is not available, it can be substituted with binding ingredients such as sticky rice, or a mixture of egg and flour.

AUTUMN

약밥
Yak-bap
Sweet glutinous rice with nuts and jujube

Yak-bap is made by mixing ingredients such as chestnuts, dried dates (*jujubes*) and pine nuts with sticky rice that has been cooked al dente, then glazing it with honey, soy sauce and sesame oil. It is also known as *yak-ban*, which literally means 'medicinal rice' or simply 'honey rice'. To achieve the ideal texture for *yak-bap*, less water is used during cooking so the grains remain firm and slightly crunchy. Historically, the term 'medicine' was often applied to foods containing honey, as honey was considered both precious and beneficial to health. *Yak-bap* was traditionally made on the 15th day of the lunar New Year, served to guests, shared with neighbours, or presented during *jesa*, a memorial service honouring ancestors.

Ingredients
420 g (3 cups) glutinous rice
10 chestnuts
15 dried Korean dates (*jujubes*)
135 g (4 ¾ oz) brown sugar
2 tbsps soy sauce
1 tbsp Korean soy sauce (*guk-ganjang*)
2 tbsps date paste
4 tbsps sesame oil
2 tbsps honey
½ tsp cinnamon powder
2 tbsps pine nuts

Date paste
300 g (10½ oz) dried Korean dates

Seasoning for chestnuts and dates
160 ml (⅔ cup) water
2 tbsps brown sugar

Making the date paste
- Rinse the Korean dates (*jujubes*) with water. Place them in a pot with plenty of water and simmer over a medium heat. Strain through a medium sieve to remove skins and seeds.

Making the chestnut and dates compote
- Peel both the outer shell and the inner skin of the chestnuts, then divide into 3 equal parts. Pit the Korean dates and cut in half.
- Put water and sugar in a pan. Once it comes to a boil, add the chestnuts and dates, and simmer until half-cooked.

Method
- Rinse the glutinous rice thoroughly and remove any impurities. Soak in water for at least 5 hours, then drain well.
- Line a steamer with a cotton cloth and steam the rice until tender, about 40 minutes.
- While the steamed glutinous rice is still hot, spread it out in a wide plate. Add brown sugar and mix evenly, then season with soy sauce, Korean soy sauce (*guk-ganjang*) and the date paste. Return the mixture to a preheated steamer and steam for about 30 minutes.* Add the stewed chestnuts and dates halfway through the steaming process.
- Once removed from the steamer, add honey, cinnamon powder and pine nuts to the rice, and mix evenly by hand.

* When steaming the seasoned sticky rice for the second time, you can choose to cover it with flour dough. The dough prevents condensation from the steamer lid dripping onto the food.

AUTUMN

개성보김치
Gaeseong-bo-kimchi
Gaeseong wrapped kimchi

'The wrapped *kimchi* in the brass bowl looked like a big rose with many layers of petals that is yet to bloom...' comes from *Unforgettable*, a novel by Park Wan-seo. *Bo-kimchi* is a delicately wrapped variety made by stuffing luxurious ingredients – such as octopus, abalone, oysters, *seogi* mushrooms, Korean pear and chestnuts – into a cabbage leaf and bundling it tightly with one of the cabbage's outer green leaves. This elegant *kimchi* is lightly seasoned, which gives it a clean, refreshing taste. However, due to its mildness, it ferments quickly and can become sour and watery in a short time. *Bo-kimchi* is not intended for long-term preservation, but rather for enjoying fresh at its peak.

Ingredients
3 heads of napa cabbage
2 Korean radishes
8 L (8½ qts) water
600 g (1 lb 5⅛ oz) coarse salt

Kimchi filling ingredients
3 abalones
2 octopuses
1 Korean pear
1 apple
80 g (2¾ oz) spring onion (scallion)
80 g (2¾ oz) water celery
80 g (2¾ oz) leaf mustard

Garnish
5 chestnuts
10 dried Korean dates (*jujubes*)
10 g (⅓ oz) rock ear mushrooms (*seogi-beoseot*)
2 tbsps pine nuts
30 g (1 oz) ginkgo nuts

Seasoning for the radish strips
150 g (5¼ oz) Korean chilli powder
salt
80 g (2¾ oz) *saeujeot* (fermented prawn/shrimp)
3 tbsps crushed garlic
1 tbsp minced ginger
60 g (2 oz) rice starch (as a thickener)
½ tbsp sugar

Kimchi juice
1 Korean pear
½ Korean radish
2 tbsps *saeujeot*
coarse salt

Recipe continues on next page

개성보김치
Gaeseong-bo-kimchi

Salting the cabbage and the radish
- Peel off the green outer leaves of the cabbage, cut it in half lengthwise, soak in salted water and drain. Sprinkle coarse salt on the thick stems, then pour salted water over the outside of the cabbage and soak. Pickle the green outer leaves separately and set aside.
- Once the cabbage is properly salted, rinse thoroughly, drain in a colander, cut into 4 cm (1½ in.) long pieces, and set them aside on a tray.
- Cut half the radish into 4 cm (1½) long rounds, then julienne.
- Cut the remaining radish into 3 cm (1¼ in.) long rounds. Make a shallow crosshatch by scoring one row into the first 2 cm (¾ in.) and a second row perpendicular to the first. Salt with coarse salt.

Preparing the fillings
- Wash the abalones thoroughly, separate the flesh from the shell and slice thinly.
- Remove the innards from the head of the octopus, peel the skin from the legs, and cut into 3 cm (1¼ in.) long pieces.
- Cut the pear and apple into small, thin squares. Trim the spring onion (scallion), water celery and leaf mustard, then cut into 3 cm (1¼ in.) long pieces.
- Combine the Korean chilli powder with the julienned radish to coat it evenly in red, and season with salt and pounded *saeujeot* (fermented prawn/shrimp).
- Grind the remaining radish and pear, combine with the seasoned radish strips, then add garlic, ginger, rice starch and sugar. Mix thoroughly.

Preparing the garnish
- Peel the chestnuts and slice them into thin strips.
- Make a vertical cut along one side of each date, remove the pits, spread them open and cut into strips.
- Soak the rock ear mushrooms (*seogi-beoseot*) in warm water, wash thoroughly and slice thinly.

Wrapping with kimchi
- Prepare a bowl of an appropriate size and line the bottom with 3 to 4 green outer leaves, with the stems facing down.
- Place the cabbage pieces vertically inside the bowl and coat each leaf alternately with the radish strips, pear and apple.
- Add the abalone, octopus, water celery, spring onion and leaf mustard.
- Garnish with chestnuts, dates, rock ear mushrooms, pine nuts and ginkgo nuts, then wrap securely with the outer leaves.

Adding the juice
- Juice the pear and radish. Mix the juice with water and season with salted prawns (shrimp). Add salt if additional seasoning is needed.
- Place the *bo-kimchi* in a container and pour in enough juice to fully submerge it.

AUTUMN

밤전
Bam-jeon
Chestnut pancake

Goryeo's chestnuts were renowned for being fleshy, sweet and juicy. It was said they were often as big as a peach. In autumn, when the chestnuts reach their peak sweetness, slice them thinly to make chestnut pancakes – a delightful dish that will surely whet your appetite.

Ingredients
15 chestnuts
125 g (1 cup) flour
160 ml (⅔ cup) water
salt

Method
- Peel the chestnuts. Cut 10 chestnuts into thin slices, and grate the remaining ones using a grater.
- Pour water into the flour, knead and season with salt.
- Mix the chestnuts slices with the grated chestnuts. Gradually add the flour batter and combine well.
- Heat oil in a pan. Scoop the mixture one by one, pressing it flat as you fry until golden brown.

밤전

개성약과와 만두과
Gaeseong yakgwa and mandu-gwa
Deep fried pastries coated with syrup

Yumil-gwa is a traditional sweet made by mixing flour with sesame oil, honey and *cheongju* (Korean rice wine), then deep-frying it in oil. Originally served as court food and ceremonial food, it was further developed in Gaeseong, the capital of Goryeo, and Hanyang, the capital of Joseon. Gaeseong's *yakgwa* boasts an interesting texture and rich ginger aroma. It is both crispy and chewy, and melts in the mouth. *Mandu-gwa* is a variation made by putting a date filling into the *yakgwa* dough, shaping it into small dumplings and frying. *Yakgwa* was often used to decorate dishes served at feasts or court events in Korea.

Gaeseong yakgwa (Gaeseong honey cookie)
400 g (2½ cups) flour
3 tbsps sesame oil
4 tbsps grapeseed oil
5 tbsps honey
6 tbsps *cheongju* (Korean rice wine)
salt

Jipcheong
100 g (3½ oz) grated ginger
50 g (1¾ oz) sugar
3½ tbsps water
300 g (10½ oz) honey

Method
- Mix the flour with salt, then add the sesame oil and grapeseed oil. Mix evenly by hand, and then pass through a sieve. Add the honey and *cheongju* (Korean rice wine), and knead until the powder is no longer visible, forming a large lump.
- Cut the dough in half and press it to form another loaf. Cut it in half again and stack the pieces on top of each other.
- Roll the dough with a rolling pin until it reaches a thickness of 0.8 cm (⅓ in.). Then, cut into 3 cm (1¼ in.) squares and score them at the centre.
- Fry the cookie squares in oil at a low temperature of 100ºC (210ºF). Put the dough in the oil and let it stand until it floats. Then, slightly increase the heat until it turns light brown.
- Once it turns light brown, flip the *yakgwa* over and fry until it is evenly coloured. The process of thoroughly draining the oil through a sieve is important.
- Add the sugar and water to the grated ginger, boil for about 5 minutes, then cool and add the honey to make the ginger-infused syrup.
- Soak the oil-drained cookies in the syrup for about 3 hours, then place them on a sieve to let the syrup drain.

Recipe continues on next page

Mandu-gwa (dumpling-shaped honey cookie)
400 g (2½ cups) flour
3 tbsps sesame oil
3 tbsps grapeseed oil
6 tbsps honey
4 tbsps ginger juice
5 tbsps *cheongju*
salt

Date filling
10 dried Korean dates (*jujubes*)
honey
cinnamon powder

Jipcheong
100 g (3½ oz) grated ginger
50 g (1¾ oz) sugar
3½ tbsps water
300 g (10½ oz) honey

Method
- Mix the flour with salt, add the sesame oil and the grapeseed oil, mix evenly with your hands, and then pass through a sieve. Add the honey, ginger juice and *cheongju*, and knead until the powder is no longer visible. Form into a large lump.
- Pit the Korean dates (*jujubes*), chop them finely, add the honey and cinnamon powder, and mix to make the date filling.
- Take a small piece of dough, the size of a chestnut, and make a well in the centre. Fill with the date mixture and press to seal it closed. Use your fingers to fold tiny pleats along the edge.
- Slowly fry at a temperature of 140°C (280°F) until light brown. The process of thoroughly draining the oil is important.
- Add the sugar and water to the grated ginger, boil for about 5 minutes, then cool and add the honey to make the ginger-infused syrup.
- Soak the oil-drained cookies in the syrup for about 1 hour, then place them on a sieve to let the syrup drain.

The Intricacy and Refinement of Goryeo Aesthetics

Geukjeonggyo
Of the utmost intricacy

Jieoseomnyeo
Exceedingly refined and beautiful

You Hong June
Advisor to the Arumjigi Culture Keepers Foundation and former Head of the Cultural Heritage Administration (Minister-designate for Culture, Sports and Tourism)

The Representation of the Goryeo Dynasty

The Goryeo dynasty (918–1392) lasted for 475 years. The survival of a single dynasty for nearly 500 years indicates a corresponding stability in terms of its political, economic, social and cultural foundation. However, Goryeo is often seen as a kingdom that was fraught with incessant warfare.

Goryeo was in fact invaded three times by the Liao dynasty over a period of 30 years during the 11th century, once by the Jin dynasty in the 12th century, and numerous times by the Mongol empire in the 13th century. In the 14th century, the kingdom eventually fell under Yuan rule for a span of 70 years and came to the end of its lifespan due to the Red Turban invasions and a surge in Japanese invaders. Such circumstances hardly seem conducive to cultural advancement.

However, this particular take on Goryeo history reduces it to the misfortunes of the Korean peninsula alone, a view altogether revised when one takes in the broader comings and goings on the East Asian stage at the time. Over the 475 years of the Goryeo dynasty, current day China saw the rise and fall of six dynasties – the Liao dynasty of the Khitan people (916–1125), the Northern Song dynasty of the Han Chinese (960–1127), the Jin dynasty of the Jurchen people (1115–1234), the Southern Song dynasty of the Han Chinese (1127–1279), the Yuan dynasty of the Mongols (1271–1368), and the Ming dynasty of the Han Chinese (1368–1644). In a sense, it was a triumph that Goryeo managed to keep its dynasty intact despite the ongoing warfare and turbulence throughout East Asia.

Goryeo's hardiness as a nation derived from its diplomacy, military and the spirit of its people. It defended itself against the first Khitan invasion thanks to Seo Hee's diplomatic ingenuity and drove back the third with the military might of Kang Gamchan. The people of Goryeo launched seven different grassroots campaigns against the invading Mongols for a full 27 years, the end result of such tenacious resistance being that Goryeo became a vassal state of the Yuan dynasty through marriage and thereby preserved its own line of kings instead of capitulating outright to the rule of the Khan. While this was perhaps a point of degradation for the people of Goryeo, internationally speaking, it did at the same time endow Goryeo with the status befitting a so-called son-in-law kingdom of the great Yuan empire instead of relegating it to the position of a mere colony.

As a matter of course, war and peace with numerous kingdoms throughout East Asia imbued Goryeo with a cosmopolitan and open-minded constitution. One result of this influence was that many Chinese people gained employment as high-ranking officials in the early Goryeo period. During the reign of King Gwangjong (949–975), Shuang Ji, who came to Goryeo as an envoy of the later Zhou dynasty, became a naturalized citizen of the kingdom. Shuang Ji proposed the implementation of the civil service examination (*gwageo jedo*) which enabled his father Shuang Zhe to be appointed as a councillor, as were Cai Renfan under King Gwangjong and Zhou Zhu under King Mokjong (997–1009).

In the face of East Asian upheaval, Goryeo chose to allow widespread naturalization for foreigners, giving them Goryeo family names and spaces in which to settle. Goryeo's inclusive open-door policy bore fruit and the ancestors of no fewer than 200 family names were all naturalized during this period, including the Chinese Shin family of Geochang, the Mongol In family of Yeonan, the Jurchen Lee family of Cheonghae, the Uyghur Seol family of Gyeongju and Jang family of Deoksu, and the Vietnamese Lee family of Hwasan. Goryeo likewise succeeded in having the name 'Korea' clearly labelled on the world map thanks to engaging in commerce with Arab merchants.

Goryeo Culture from an International Perspective
During times of peace, Goryeo matured and gained cosmopolitan sophistication through its robust cultural interactions with other East Asian nations. In the case of the *Tripitaka Koreana*, three versions of the sacred scriptures were made – one each for the Song dynasty, Liao dynasty and Goryeo dynasty. Work on the *Tripitaka Koreana* began in 1011, with the first edition completed 76 years later (1087) being the Northern Song version. The Liao edition begun in 1031 and completed over a period of 23 years was the Khitan version (1054). The second edition of the *Tripitaka Koreana* (1251), intended to ward off the Mongol invasion through Buddhist piety, was produced on Ganghwa Island for 15 years from 1236 onwards. This edition constitutes the Goryeo version of the scripts and its original plates are currently housed at Haein Temple.

The ingenuity and sophistication of Goryeo culture gained international recognition. The rich cultural heritage of the Goryeo period – metal type casting, celadon, metal craft, mother-of-pearl lacquerwork, Buddhist paintings, sutra transcripts and more – offers us proof of this fact in the most concrete terms. We also see Chinese records which attest to the superb beauty of Goryeo artwork.

In his history of painting entitled *Examination of Painting (Hua Jian)*, Tang Hou of the Yuan dynasty covers foreign paintings and says, 'The Avalokitesvara paintings of Goryeo exemplify excellent craftsmanship. They have their roots in the work of Tang dynasty painter Yuchi Yiseng, whose artistic intent has been passed down and reached new heights of refinement and ornateness,' using the expression *jieoseomnyeo* (exceedingly refined and beautiful) in his assessment.

Xu Jing, who came to Goryeo as an attendant to the Song dynasty envoy during the first year of King Injong's reign (1123), drew up an illustrated report for Emperor Huizong on the various aspects of Goryeo culture which he encountered over the course of his stay. The *Illustrated Account of the Embassy to Goryeo in the Xuanhe Era (Xuanhe Fengshi Gaoli Tujing)* is already well-known for its records of how the people of Goryeo referred to the celadon that they produced as jade-green in hue. In his entry on cavalry horses, Xu Jing opines that 'the saddles for the cavalry are made of mother-of-pearl and are extremely intricate', using the expression *geukjeonggyo* (of the utmost intricacy). His entry on local products notes that 'the mother-of-pearl craftsmanship is so detailed and intricate that it is rendered a treasure', using the expression *semilgagwi* (exquisite and precious).

Due to its remarkable detail and intricacy, Goryeo's mother-of-pearl lacquerwork was in fact exported to current day China. The Yuan empress requested a mother-of-pearl lacquer sutra case from Goryeo, which, in the 13th year of the reign of King Wonjong (1272), prompted the installation of a government office dedicated to the production of sutra cases. *On Lacquer Decoration (Xiushilu)*, a book on lacquerwork written during the Ming dynasty by Huang Dacheng, also mentions Goryeo mother-of-pearl lacquerwork making its way to the Great Ming.

The Beauty and Value of Goryeo Culture
In 2015, the Leeum Museum of Art held a special exhibition titled *Exquisite and Precious: The Splendor of Korean Art*. If we were to borrow from the characteristics of Goryeo art to summarize the details of Korean art represented in the expression *semilgagwi* (exquisite and precious), we would find our way to an intricate and refined sense of beauty, namely that of *geukjeonggyo* (of the utmost intricacy) and *jieoseomnyeo* (exceedingly refined and beautiful).

The celadon, metal craft, mother-of-pearl lacquerwork and Buddhist paintings made during the Goryeo period all embody these very traits. We will here examine the lesser-known example of the metalwork dress ornament. Two centimetres in width and three centimetres in height, this dainty little ornament tended to be produced in pairs and wrought for the most part out of pure gold, gilt bronze, silver and occasionally jade. Many of the ornaments were in the shape of spheres, squares and flower buds. The pattern work featured flora such as lotuses and peonies in exquisite combination with fauna such as cranes, mandarin ducks, mallards, phoenixes, dragons, turtles, fish, bees and butterflies, but at times consisted of Buddhist iconography along the lines of the Four Heavenly Kings.

We see these attributes reflected in the hundreds of Goryeo ornaments preserved at the National Museum of Korea and the Ewha Womans University Museum, as well as the dozens overseas at institutions such as the Musée national des arts asiatiques-Guimet in France and the Metropolitan Museum of Art in New York, not to mention the few which belong to private collections.

Nevertheless, these items continued to be handed down without a consensus as to their purpose until they were finally revealed to be dress ornaments through the 1999 discovery of a silver pair placed on the bosom of the remains excavated from a burial mound in the Myeongam area of Cheongju. Given the intricate and refined nature of these ornaments created by hammering out metal sheets on both sides and carving them with openwork patterns, we can only imagine how elaborate and beautiful the clothing that they adorned must have been. This was likely the very pinnacle of *geukjeonggyo* (of the utmost intricacy) and *jieoseomnyeo* (exceedingly refined and beautiful).

When covering the 15th year of the reign of King Onjo (4 BC) in the *Baekje Annals (Baekjebongi)* of *The History of the Three Kingdoms (Samguksagi)*, Goryeo period Confucian scholar Kim Busik draws on the expression *geomibullu hwaibulchi* to describe modesty that falls not into squalor and magnificence that turns not into excess. *The Administrative Code of Joseon (Joseongyeonggukjeon)*, written by Jeong Dojeon as the conceptual blueprint for the Joseon dynasty, refers to the same concept, albeit using different language. As a superlative precis of the aesthetics of the *Three Kingdoms (Samguk)* and Joseon periods, the standard of *geomibullu hwaibulchi* has stirred up a comprehensive sense of affinity and proved a key concept and source of cultural inspiration in terms of better grasping our aesthetic objectives.

What aesthetic values, then, has Goryeo culture instilled in us? What frame of mind from this period warrants bequeathal to the next generation? Once again, the answer to these questions can be found in the integrity behind the intricate and refined beauty of Goryeo – that is, the aesthetics of *geukjeonggyo* (of the utmost intricacy) and *jieoseomnyeo* (exceedingly refined and beautiful) – as well as the artisan's mentality through which such an aesthetic comes into being.

They say that 'a masterpiece is beautiful in its details' and that 'God is in the details'. Precision of detail as the result of intricate and painstaking labour is itself a thing of beauty. This degree of detail can only be achieved through exhaustive and assiduous discipline, which is no different from an artisan's mentality that takes full responsibility for the workings of one's mind and hands. The free-spirited, cosmopolitan nature and the exquisite, intricate beauty of Goryeo aesthetics provide us with a valuable source of inspiration and a guiding principle for cultural innovation in an era that demands a meticulous and unwavering artisan mentality. Far from being a mere buzzword referencing the past, this rendition of Goryeo aesthetics awakens our awareness of the creative foundations embedded in our Goryeo heritage and strengthens our resolve to preserve and protect it.

Pages 174–75:
Goryeo celadons

Right:
Three-spined shore crabs (*Bang-ge*)

겨울

WINTER

returning to root

WINTER

연계길경온반
Yeongye-gilgyeong-on-ban
Rice with chicken and doraji

Old Korean cookbooks record a wide variety of chicken dishes, and among them, those made with young birds often use the term *yeongye*, meaning 'young chicken'. Inspired by a traditional soup once enjoyed by noble families, Onjium presents a comforting rice soup made with tender young chicken.

Ingredients
360 g (2 cups) rice
1 chicken
200 g (7 oz) fresh *doraji* (bellflower root), peeled and cut in half
100 g (3½ oz) *deodeok* (lance asiabell roots), peeled
5 *toran* (taro), peeled
2 potatoes
2 tbsps spring onion (scallion), chopped
1 tbsp crushed garlic
salt

Chicken broth ingredients
30 g (1 oz) ginger
10 g (⅓ oz) peppercorns
30 g (1 oz) spring onion
50 g (1¾ oz) onion
50 g (1¾ oz) *doraji*

Method
- Rinse the rice and soak in water for 30 minutes before cooking. Set aside the water used to rinse the rice for later.
- Soak chicken in cold water to remove blood. Blanch the chicken briefly in boiling water, then remove immediately. Bring a fresh pan of water to a boil. Add the chicken along with the ingredients for chicken broth. Simmer for 40 minutes. Remove the chicken from the stock and set aside. Take out all the vegetables from the stock as well. Return the chicken bones to the pot and simmer the stock for another 30 minutes. Strain the stock through a muslin to obtain a clear broth. Season with salt. Place chopped spring onion (scallion) and minced garlic in a fine mesh pouch and steep in the broth.
- Parboil the *toran* (taro) in the water used to rinse rice, cooking them only halfway.
- Grate the potatoes and squeeze out the excess water. Set aside the water to get settled starch. Allow the extracted liquid to settle and use the starch that collects at the bottom. Mix the starch back into the grated potatoes to form a dough. Shape into small balls.
- Add the *doraji* (bellflower root), *deodeok* (lance asiabell roots), *toran* and potato balls to the chicken stock and boil for 20 minutes.
- Scoop rice into a bowl. Arrange the cooked vegetables and potato balls over the rice. Pour in the hot broth and top with the chopped spring onion.

연계길경온반
Yeongye-gilgyeong-on-ban

WINTER

매생이전복탕
Maesaengi-jeonbok-tang
Abalone and maeseangi seaweed soup

Seaweed known as *maesaengi* is harvested from the pristine waters off the south coast of Korea. Resembling a skein of green thread, *maesaengi* has a texture and appearance similar to green laver. It is commonly boiled with oysters to make a nourishing soup. When combined with tender steamed abalone and a rich, flavourful stock, this dish becomes a wholesome winter delicacy that captures the essence of the sea.

Ingredients
5 abalones
1 stalk of spring onion (scallion)
50 g (1¾ oz) *maesaengi* seaweed
3 g (1 tsp) starch
2 tbsps perilla seed oil
3 tbsps *cheongju* (Korean rice wine)

Beef brisket soup
600 ml (2½ cups) beef brisket broth
1 tsp chopped spring onion
½ tsp crushed garlic
Korean soy sauce (*guk-ganjang*)
salt
salted anchovy sauce

Method
- Place the abalone shell-side down in a basket set over boiling water. Drizzle *cheongju* (Korean rice wine) over the abalone, top with spring onion (scallion) and steam for 1½ hours.
- Remove the abalone meat from the shells and cut into bite-sized pieces.
- Coat a frying pan with perilla seed oil and sauté the *maesaengi* until it turns green.
- Place the spring onion and garlic in a fine sieve and brew in the beef brisket broth. Season the broth with Korean soy sauce (*guk-ganjang*), salt and anchovy sauce.
- Dissolve the starch in a cup of water.
- Add the *maesaengi* to the seasoned beef broth and bring to a boil. Once it starts boiling, stir in the starch liquid to thicken.
- Place the abalone in a bowl and pour the beef brisket soup over it.

WINTER

어만두 누르미
Eo-mandu nureumi
Fish dumpling drizzled with nureumi sauce

Nureumi refers to a traditional dish made by pouring a starch-based sauce over stewed or broiled main ingredients. Inspired by this classic recipe, Onjium has created a modern version using fish fillet as a dumpling wrapper, finished with a drizzle of starch sauce. If the fish fillet is too moist, it can easily break. To prevent this, allow the fish to rest at room temperature for about 20 minutes to let excess moisture evaporate.

Ingredients
300 g (10½ oz) cod fillet
salt
2 tbsps starch

Dumpling filling
1 snow crab
½ courgette (zucchini), deseeded and cut into matchsticks 3 cm (1⅛ in.) long
70 g (2½ oz) onion, chopped
70 g (2½ oz) tofu
½ tbsp chopped spring onion (scallion)
½ tsp crushed garlic
½ tsp roasted sesame seeds
1 tsp sesame oil
½ tsp salt

Nureumi sauce
1 tbsp flour
100 ml (⅖ cup) water
salt
Sichuan pepper

Method
- Slice the cod fillet into 7 cm (2¾ in.) squares. Sprinkle with salt. Spread the pieces over a wicker tray and let them dry for about 1 hour.
- Make the filling. Steam the crab for 15 minutes over boiling water. Remove the meat from the crab. Sprinkle the courgette (zucchini) with salt and let it rest for 30 minutes. Squeeze out excess water. Stir-fry in a frying pan. Add the chopped spring onion (scallion), crushed garlic, roasted sesame seeds and sesame oil. Set aside.
- Stir-fry the onion in the frying pan. Squeeze out excess water from the tofu and crush. Combine all the ingredients. Season with salt.
- Coat the cod squares with starch flour. Place a tablespoon of the dumpling filling on each of the squares. Wrap and roll.
- Prepare the *nureumi* sauce. Stir the flour into the water until smooth and bring to a gentle boil. Add the salt and Sichuan pepper to finish.
- Steam the dumplings for 5 minutes over boiling water. Place the dumplings on a plate. Drizzle the *nureumi* sauce over the dumplings.

WINTER

벚굴냉채
Beotgul-naengchae
Cold beotgul oyster salad

Beotgul oysters occur naturally in the waters of estuaries. As they are not cultivated, they can only be harvested in winter. Onjium presents a chilled *beotgul* oyster salad, dressed with a blend of clear fish sauce and lemon juice. The oyster shells can be used as serving vessels for an elegant presentation.

Ingredients
4 *beotgul* oysters
3 *bidan-meongge* (a type of sea pineapple)
¾ Korean pear
4 chestnuts
20 g (¾ oz) *minari* (Korean watercress), cut into 3 cm (1¼ in.) lengths
1 dried red pepper
3 *seogi* mushrooms
fish sauce
salted anchovy sauce
lemon juice

Garlic sauce
1 tbsp brown rice vinegar
½ tsp crushed garlic
½ tsp sugar
pinch of salt
1 tsp lemon juice

Sweet vinegar water
1 tbsp vinegar
1 tbsp sugar
1 tbsp cooking wine
4 tbsps water
½ tsp salt

Method
- Remove the oysters from the shells. Cut each into 3 or 4 pieces.
- Cut the hard shell of each *bidan-meongge* (sea pineapple) open to reach the edible flesh. Cut into bite-sized pieces.
- Cut the pear into 8 equal parts. Peel and slice diagonally into bite-sized pieces. Peel the inner skin of the chestnuts and cut into discs.
- Cut the dried red pepper in half. Remove the seeds. Tear by hand into natural shreds.
- Soak the *seogi* mushrooms in water and strain. Tear by hand as with the dried red pepper.
- Marinate the oysters in the garlic sauce for 10 minutes.
- Marinate the pear, chestnut and *minari* (Korean watercress) in sweet vinegar water for 10 minutes.
- Combine all the ingredients together and toss with fish sauce to serve.

벚굴냉채
Beotgul-naengchae

WINTER

설야멱적
Seolya-myeok-jeok
Grilled and lightly marinated beef

An old book refers to *seolya-jeok* as a beef dish. According to a historical recipe, beef was seasoned with oil and spicy vegetables, then grilled rare. It was then soaked in cold water before being grilled again over high charcoal heat. The secret is soaking the beef in cold water to make it tender. Onjium's version involves quickly grilling beef – previously marinated in pear juice – at a high heat over charcoal to sear the surface, then marinating the beef in seasoning and grilling it once more. This two-step process makes the beef very tender.

Ingredients
500 g (1 lb 1⅝ oz) beef sirloin
240 ml (1 cup) Korean pear juice
ground pine nuts

Seasoning for the beef
2½ tbsps soy sauce
1 tbsp sugar
1 tbsp honey
2½ tbsps chopped onion
1 tbsp spring onion (scallion)
⅔ tbsp crushed garlic
1 tbsp sesame oil
1 tbsp grapeseed oil
1 tbsp ground roasted sesame seeds
pepper

Method
- Remove the fat from the beef. Cut the beef into thick slices. Soak in pear juice for 1 hour to remove any blood.
- On the barbecue, grill the beef on a grate at a high heat over charcoal, searing it until just rare.
- Marinate the beef in seasoning for 1 hour.
- Grill the beef once more over charcoal on the barbecue. Cut the beef into bite-sized pieces. Arrange on a serving plate and sprinkle with ground pine nuts.

설야멱적

WINTER

홍합시래기무밥
Honghap-siraegi-mu-bap
Rice with dried radish leaves and mussels

White radish leaves dried in autumn, known as *siraegi* in Korean, are rich in dietary fibre and vitamins. Traditionally, Koreans consume essential nutrients during winter by cooking rice with *siraegi* prepared in the autumn. Both white radish and mussels are most delicious in winter. At Onjium, white radish and mussels are added to *siraegi* seasoned with perilla seed oil, then cooked with rice in mussel stock – creating a seasonal delicacy.

Ingredients
360 g (2 cups) of rice
150 g (5¼ oz) mussels
80 g (2¾ oz) *siraegi* (dried radish green)
200 g (7 oz) white radish, peeled and shredded
720 ml (3 cups) water

Seasoning for the siraegi (dried radish green)
Korean soy sauce (*guk-ganjang*)
chopped spring onion (scallion)
crushed garlic
perilla seed oil

Method
- Soak the rice in water for 30 minutes.
- Parboil the mussels. Set aside the water used to parboil the mussels.
- Soak the *siraegi* (dried radish green) in water for 10 minutes and strain. Boil for 40 minutes at low heat until tender. Peel the hard parts of the leaves. Cut into pieces 3 cm (1¼ in.) long. Mix with the seasoning and stir-fry. Stir-fry the radish.
- Combine the parboiled mussel water, *siraegi* and rice in a pan. Bring to a boil, then reduce the heat to low and simmer for about 10 minutes. Add the meat of the mussels and white radish. Turn off the heat and let the rice stand, covered, for 15 minutes without opening the lid.

WINTER

우엉잡채
Ueong-japchae
Stir-fried ueong and sweet potato noodles

Many recipes in old cookbooks include dish names with the prefix *jap*, which means 'to mix'. *Japchae* refers to a dish made by combining various vegetables. Onjium presents a modern take on *japchae* using noodles made from crispy root vegetables. This version features finely shredded burdock root (*ueong*) and lotus root stir-fried with sweet potato starch noodles and seasoned with soy sauce.

Ingredients
½ stalk burdock (*ueong*), peeled and finely shredded
1 lotus root, peeled and finely shredded
2 hot green peppers, deseeded and finely shredded
½ hot red pepper, deseeded and finely shredded
50 g (1¾ oz) dried *euni* mushrooms
50 g (1¾ oz) sweet potato starch noodle
salt
sesame oil

Seasoning
soy sauce
salt
raw sugar
crushed garlic
perilla seed oil

Method
- Soak the burdock (*ueong*) in vinegar water to prevent the colour from browning. Strain and parboil. Stir-fry, adding seasoning.
- Parboil the lotus root in boiling water. Stir-fry, adding seasoning.
- Stir-fry the green and red peppers separately.
- Soak the *euni* mushrooms in water. Cut into bite-sized pieces. Season with salt and sesame oil. Stir-fry.
- Soak the noodles in water. Strain and cook in boiling water. Rinse in cold water, rubbing the noodles with hands to remove starch thoroughly.
- Coat a frying pan with oil. Stir-fry the noodles. Season the noodles to your taste. Combine the burdock, lotus root, peppers, noodles and the mushrooms, and stir-fry all together. Place in a bowl to serve.

WINTER

온반
Onban
Hot soup with rice

Koreans traditionally enjoyed hot soup topped with an assortment of meats and vegetables. The stock could be made from various meats, including beef and chicken, while the garnishes often featured ingredients such as cod and pufferfish. At Onjium, the stock is made using the navel end of beef brisket.

Ingredients
360 g (2 cups) rice, rinsed and cooked
1 kg (2 lbs 4 oz) brisket navel end
200 g (7 oz) bean sprouts, tails removed
150 g (5¼ oz) oyster mushrooms (*neutari-beoseot*)
90 g (½ cup) mung beans, soaked in water for 4 hours
30 g (1 oz) *minari* (Korean watercress),
    cut into 3 cm (1¼ in.) lengths
1 egg
30 g (1 oz) chopped spring onion (scallion)
crushed garlic
Korean soy sauce (*guk-ganjang*)
salt

Method
- Make stock with the beef brisket. Remove the meat from the stock. Let it cool. Put the chopped spring onion (scallion) and crushed garlic over a sieve and brew in the stock. Season the stock with Korean soy sauce (*guk-ganjang*) and salt.
- Parboil the bean sprouts in salted water. Parboil the oyster mushrooms (*neutari-beoseot*). Skin the mung beans by rubbing with your hands. Grind the beans in a mixer. Season with salt. Scoop the bean paste into bite-sized pancake shapes and griddle. Set aside. Skewer the *minari* (Korean watercress). Dip in egg yolk and griddle.
- Cut the cooled meat into thin slices.
- Put the rice in a bowl. Top the rice with the meat and other ingredients. Pour over the stock. Serve hot.

WINTER

떡만둣국
Tteok-mandu-guk
Rice cake soup with dumplings

Dumplings are a traditional winter food. In the past, the royal court enjoyed soup made with crescent-shaped dumplings called *byeongsi*, which were folded in half rather than rolled in wrinkly wrappers. Onjium recreates this winter dish with smooth, crescent-shaped dumplings and rice cakes, all served in a rich beef brisket broth.

Ingredients
200 g (7 oz) sliced rice cakes
⅓ spring onion (scallion)
1 egg
beef brisket broth
crushed garlic
Korean soy sauce (*guk-ganjang*)
salt
dried, shredded red pepper

Dumpling wrapper dough
150 g (1¼ cups) flour
salt
½ tbsp egg white
½ tbsp grapeseed oil
50 ml (¼ cup) water

Dumpling filling
100 g (3½ oz) napa cabbage *kimchi*
100 g (3½ oz) mung bean sprouts
70 g (2½ oz) beef bottom round
2 dried shiitake mushrooms
50 g (1¾ oz) tofu
sesame oil
ground sesame
salt

Seasoning for the beef and shiitake mushrooms
soy sauce
sugar
chopped spring onion
crushed garlic
ground sesames
sesame oil

Method
- Make the dough for the dumpling wrappers. Wrap in a damp cotton cloth. Let it rest in the refrigerator overnight.
- Prepare the dumpling filling. Squeeze excess liquid from the *kimchi*, then chop and mix it with sesame oil and ground sesame seeds. Parboil the mung bean sprouts. Squeeze out excess water and chop finely. Mince the meat and mix with seasoning. Take a small amount and make small meatballs. Soak the shiitake mushrooms in water for 20 minutes, strain, squeeze excess water, shred and season. Mash the tofu, then wrap in a cotton cloth and squeeze out moisture. Mix all the ingredients. Season with salt.
- Place the dough on a cutting board and divide into 10 equal-sized pieces. Roll each piece out with a rolling pin into 7 cm (2¾ in.) discs.
- Place a spoonful of filling in the centre of each disc. Fold each disc in half over the filling and press the edges together to seal.
- Separate the egg white and yolk. Pan-fry each into thin omelettes then cut into small discs. Put the meatball in the centre and fold in half over the filling to garnish.
- Put the dumplings and rice cakes in beef stock and bring to a boil. Brew the crushed garlic in the stock over a sieve. Season with Korean soy sauce (*guk-ganjang*) and salt.
- When the dumplings are cooked, they will float to the surface. Add chopped spring onion (scallion).
- Scoop into bowls. Garnish with the meatballs and shredded red pepper.

WINTER

가시리볶음
Gasiri-bokeum
Stir-fried gasiri seaweed

Gasiri seaweed is named after *gasi*, meaning thorns in Korean, as it looks like thorns. Onjium uses *gasiri* harvested only in small amounts on Gureop-do Island. *Gasiri* is cleaned thoroughly to remove the salt, and dried before stir-frying or deep-frying. This makes for a very delicious and crispy seaweed dish.

Ingredients
50 g (1¾ oz) *gasiri* seaweed, dried
1 sheet laver, cut into small pieces
perilla seed oil
salt

Method
- Preheat a frying pan.
- Coat with perilla seed oil. Stir-fry the *gasiri* and laver together.
- Season with salt.

WINTER

유자주머니
Yuja-jumeoni
Yuja citron pouch

Yuja (yuzu) fruit is harvested only for a month or two in early winter. *Yuja* is made into marmalade rather than taken as fresh fruit. The fresh, sweet and unique citron flavour and aroma of *yuja* together with chewy, sweet chestnuts and Korean dates (*jujubes*) makes this pouch a very special, rich dessert. This recipe yields 20 servings.

Ingredients
5 medium-sized *yuja* (yuzu) fruits
200 g (7 oz) chestnuts, shredded
80 g (2¾ oz) dried Korean dates (*jujubes*), shredded
10 g (⅓ oz) *seogi* mushrooms, shredded
100 g (3½ oz) *yuja* fruit flesh
150 g (5¼ oz) sugar

Sugar syrup
360 g (12½ oz) sugar
400 ml (1⅔ cups) water

Method
- Wash the *yuja* (yuzu) fruits in salt water. Thinly peel the bumpy skin from the rinds. Dip in boiling water. Place each fruit on a chopping board with the stalk facing up. Make 6 vertical slits starting 1 cm (⅜ in.) from the bottom. Carefully remove the inner flesh from the rind and discard the seeds. Finely chop the fruit flesh.
- Combine the sugar and water, and simmer over a low heat to make a syrup. Allow the syrup to cool completely.
- Mix the chopped chestnuts, Korean dates (*jujubes*), mushrooms, fruit flesh and sugar to make the filling. Stuff each rind with the filling and tie the fruit closed with thread.
- Layer the filled *yuja* pouches in a jar. Pour the cooled sugar syrup into the jar until it covers the fruit. Store in the refrigerator. The *yuja* can be eaten after 1 week. Make sure the syrup covers all the fruits completely, as exposed parts may discolour.

WINTER

잣죽
Jat-juk
Pine nut porridge

Since ancient times, Korean pine nuts have been renowned internationally for their exceptional quality. Valued for their rich nutrients, pine nuts were considered medicinal and highly prized – so expensive that they were typically out of reach for common people. The ingredient appears frequently in royal court recipes. Pine nut porridge, with its creamy texture, enticing aroma and nutty flavour, is easy to digest and was often served in the royal court as a light dish to be eaten upon rising, before breakfast.

Ingredients

135 g (4¾ oz) pine nuts, preferably Korean
130 g (⅔ cup) short-grain rice, soaked in water
1.4 L (6 cups) water
chopped pine nuts, as garnish
salt or sugar

Method

- Toast the pine nuts lightly in a dry pan, then grind finely together with 240 ml (1 cup) of water using a blender.
- Rinse the rice thoroughly and soak for about 1 hour. Grind the soaked rice finely with 480 ml (2 cups) of water using a blender.
- Simmer the ground rice mixture. When it begins to thicken, add the pine nut mixture. The porridge will appear thin at first, but continue simmering over a low heat until it returns to a creamy consistency.
- Sprinkle with the chopped pine nuts to garnish. Serve with salt or sugar, according to preference.

WINTER

복어피편
Bogeo pipyeon
Pufferfish skin jelly

Pufferfish skin is rich in collagen and its broth sets into a jelly when chilled. Various ingredients are added to the *pipyeon* and encased in jelly, which is then sliced for serving. The transparent skin jelly showcases the colourful fillings, offering both visual appeal and an interesting texture. Its excellent shelf life makes it a popular dish for festive occasions. At Onjium, it is served with a coriander (cilantro) salad, acknowledging coriander's historical popularity in Gaeseong cuisine.

Ingredients
1 kg (2 lb 4 oz) pufferfish
dried kelp (*dasima*)
½ *aehobak* (a type of Korean summer squash)
2 medium-sized eggs
5 bunches spring onion (scallion)
salt
Korean soy sauce (*guk-ganjang*)
1 tbsp ginger juice
1 tbsp lemon juice

Coriander (cilantro) salad dressing
100 g (3½ oz) coriander (cilantro)
1 tbsp Korean fish sauce
1 tbsp Korean plum extract
1½ tbsps vinegar
salt

Method
- Debone the pufferfish and transfer the bones to a pot of water along with the dried kelp (*dasima*) to make the broth.
- Scale the pufferfish skin, blanch, then drain.
- Cut the pufferfish skin into julienne strips and slice the pufferfish meat thinly.
- Chop the *aehobak* (Korean summer squash) into 5 cm (2 in.) long blocks, peel each piece into one long sheet (*dolryeokkaki*) and julienne. Sprinkle with salt and let sit. Heat a pan, coat with oil and stir-fry.
- Separate the egg whites and yolks, then cook thin white and yellow crepes. Slice them into julienne strips. Chop the spring onion (scallion).
- Strain the pufferfish broth through a sieve, then add the sliced pufferfish skin and meat to the broth and bring to a boil. Season with Korean soy sauce (*guk-ganjang*), salt and ginger juice, turn off the heat and finish with a dash of lemon juice.
- Add the *aehobak* and egg crepe strips to the seasoned broth, then pour everything into a mould.
- Sprinkle with chopped spring onion and chill in the refrigerator until set.
- Cut the jelly into bite-sized pieces and serve with coriander (cilantro) salad.

Bogeo pipyeon

WINTER

어육김치냉채
Eoyuk-kimchi-naengchae
Wrapped kimchi salad with seafood

This unique cold dish takes inspiration from Gaeseong's *bo-kimchi*, or wrapped *kimchi*. Onjium's original recipe uses well-ripened *baek-kimchi* (white *kimchi*) to wrap a variety of ingredients, including octopus, abalone, boiled beef and Korean citron. Through this creation, Onjium aims to showcase the versatility of *kimchi* in a refined and unexpected way. Onjium's patrons have praised its refreshing, palate-cleansing taste – those from overseas seemed to particularly enjoy it.

Ingredients
¼ head of white *kimchi*
1 octopus
2 abalones
2 *bidan-meongge* (a type of sea pineapple)
100 g (3½ oz) lean beef, boiled until tender to be sliced
2 Korean chestnuts
¼ Korean pear
50 g (1¾ oz) Korean citron peel

For garnish
pine nuts
pieces of pitted, rolled and sliced dried Korean dates (*jujubes*)
fresh pomegranate seeds

Method
- Separate outer leaves from the heart of a well-ripened *baek-kimchi*. Reserve the wide outer *kimchi* leaves for wrapping. Slice the thick stems horizontally into thin pieces and soak them in *kimchi* sauce.

Preparing the stuffing
- Use the heart and leftovers of the white *kimchi* to make the stuffing. Chop them into 4 cm (1½ in.) long pieces, cutting the large parts in half. Also, cut the Korean radish and mustard greens inside the *kimchi*.
- Turn the head of the octopus inside out, remove the entrails, and parboil for about 1½ minutes. Chop into 4 cm (1½ in.) long pieces and let it soak in the *kimchi* juice.
- Wash the abalones thoroughly, parboil for about 2 minutes, then remove the entrails and slice thinly.
- Clean and prepare the *bidan-meongge* (sea pineapples), cutting them into 4 to 6 parts depending on the size.
- Cut the boiled beef into 0.2 cm (¹⁄₁₂ in.) thin slices.
- Peel the chestnuts, trim the corners, and cut them into 0.2 cm (¹⁄₁₂ in.) thin slices.
- Peel the pear and cut into 0.2 cm (¹⁄₁₂ in.) thin slices lengthwise, diagonally.

Stuff and wrap
- Spread the wide outer leaves of the white *kimchi*, placing the prepared ingredients neatly at the centre of each leaf.
- Make sure the *bidan-meongge*, octopus and Korean pear are placed evenly, then top with julienned citron rind. Wrap it neatly with the outer leaf into a roll.
- Soak the rolls with citron peel in the white *kimchi* juice. Chill for a day.
- Transfer each roll into a bowl, pour cold *kimchi* sauce over it and garnish.

WINTER

모둠편육
Modum-pyeonyuk
Assorted boiled cuts of meat

Boiled cuts of meat are chilled and pressed into a shape, then sliced thinly to make *pyeonyuk*. (It is called *suyuk* when sliced still hot and *pyeonyuk* when the meat is chilled and pressed before slicing.) The best cuts for this dish are those rich in collagen, from either beef or pork, as they yield a tender, slightly gelatinous texture. The people of Gaeseong preferred pork and traditionally used a ceramic steamer to enhance the flavour. Pork *pyeonyuk* was prepared with great care for special occasions.

Ingredients
1 ox head, trimmed
1 kg (2 lbs 4 oz) beef shank
1 kg (2 lbs 4 oz) beef brisket
1 kg (2 lbs 4 oz) extra fatty pork belly
dried kelp (*dasima*)
1 bunch spring onions (scallions)
100 g (3½ oz) chives
100 g (3½ oz) thin green onions

Method
- Buy a trimmed head of ox meat, remove any remaining hair, and soak in cold water for about half a day to draw out the blood.
- Also soak the beef shank, beef brisket and pork belly in cold water for about half a day to remove excess blood.
- Parboil the cuts in the following order: beef shank, beef brisket, pork belly and finally the ox head meat. Take extra time with the ox head meat.
- Put the dried kelp (*dasima*) in cold water and bring to a boil. Add the parboiled cuts of beef shank, brisket and ox head meat. Remove the beef shank and brisket after 1½ hours, and the ox head meat after 2½ hours.
- Line the bottom of a steamer pot with the spring onions (scallions), place the parboiled pork belly on top and steam for about 1½ hours.
- Let all the cuts cool, then slice neatly and arrange them on a large serving plate. Lightly steam the chives and thin green onions and serve on the side.

모둠편육

WINTER

조랭이떡볶음
Joraengitteok-bokkeum
Stir fried and marinated beef with joraengi rice cake

In Gaeseong, the Lunar New Year is celebrated with snowman-shaped rice cakes served in soup. These same rice cakes are also used to make *tteokbokki*. For this dish, marinated minced beef is stir-fried, then *joraengi* rice cakes and mushrooms are added to create a savory-sweet combination with a hint of brininess.

Joraengitteok
360 g (3 cups) short-grain rice flour
5 tbsps water

Ingredients
100 g (3½ oz) lean beef cut
beef marinade (*see *Okjamhwa-kkot-ssam*, page 148)
2 shiitake mushrooms
3 tbsps beef broth
dried rock ear mushrooms (*seogi-beoseot*)

Method
- Wet the rice flour with water and steam it in a bamboo steamer for about 20 minutes. While still hot, pound it with a pestle, then roll and stretch it into a long, thin cylinder. Use a wooden chopstick to cut and press the centre of each piece to form multiple snowman-like shaped rice cakes.
- Mince the beef by hand and marinate it in the prepared sauce.
- Cut the shiitake mushrooms into thin slices and stir-fry them in a pan.
- Stir-fry the marinated beef in a separate pan, then add the *joraengi* rice cakes. Pour in a small amount of beef broth and continue stirring. Add the stir-fried shiitake mushrooms.
- Soak the rock ear mushrooms (*seogi-beoseot*) in water, then julienne and use to garnish the dish.

WINTER

열구자탕반
Yeolguja-tang-ban
Royal hot pot with rice

There are several theories about the origin of the name *yeolguja*, but the most widely accepted is that it means 'pleasing to the mouth' (熱口子, written in Chinese characters). At Onjium, rather than serving the dish in the traditional *sinseollo* (a grand cooking device), they present it as rice in soup, a style that was popular in old Gaeseong for individual servings. *Hansik*, or Korean culinary arts, places great emphasis on the colours of food, often presenting dishes in *obangsaek* – the five colours representing the five elements in ancient Asian philosophy. This dish exemplifies that tradition, featuring colourful ingredients neatly arranged in a clean yet deeply flavourful broth.

Ingredients
500 g (1 lb 1⅝ oz) beef shank
⅓ Korean radish
⅓ carrot
500 g (1 lb 1⅝ oz) beef tripe
⅓ beef lung
2 fresh octopuses
2 fresh abalones
1 dried sea cucumber, soaked in water
4 dried shiitake mushrooms, soaked in water
2 ginkgo nuts
cheongjang (light soy sauce)
salt
sesame oil

For wanja (Korean meatballs), jidan (Korean egg crepe strips), chodae (Korean water celery skewer) and jeon (Korean fritter)
100 g (3½ oz) lean beef cut
20 g (¾ oz) tofu
4 medium-sized eggs
5 rock ear mushrooms (*seogi-beoseot*)
50 g (1¾ oz) water celery
100 g (3½ oz) cod fillet

Sauce for wanja and soup ingredients
1 tbsp minced spring onion (scallion)
1 tsp crushed garlic
1 tsp sesame oil
black pepper

Recipe continues on the next page

Making the broth with shank cut, beef tripe and lung
- Soak the shank cuts in cold water to remove blood, then parboil briefly. Transfer to a pot filled with a plenty of water for about 1½ hours to make the broth. Remove the meat and skim off any scum from the surface.
- Prepare the radish and carrot, and to the broth. Cook until tender.
- Thoroughly clean the beef tripe by skinning and parboiling it, then rinse well. Place in a pot with fresh water and boil for about 2 hours until tender. Drain and skim the broth.
- Remove blood from the lung, parboil for about 10 minutes and rinse thoroughly under running water. Boil the lung in a separate pot of water for about 2 hours.

Preparing the octopuses, abalones and sea cucumber
- Turn the head of the octopuses inside out, remove the entrails and parboil for about 2 minutes.
- Wash the shelled abalones thoroughly, dip them in boiling water, remove the entrails, and slice thinly at an angle.
- Cut the soaked sea cucumber into pieces similar in size to the abalone, season with salt and sesame oil, then pan-fry.

Making wanja, jidan, chodae and jeon
- Mince the beef, mix with the crushed tofu and meatball sauce, and knead. Roll into tiny balls 1 cm (⅜ in.) in diameter, coat with egg yolk and pan-fry.
- Take 3 eggs, separate the whites from the yolks, add salt, and make thin crepes on an oil-coated pan. When making the egg-white crepes, divide the egg whites in half and mix one half with minced rock ear mushrooms (*seogi-beoseot*) to make one sheet with them and one without.
- Take the leaves off the water celery, cut only the stem into bite-sized pieces, then skewer. Coat it with egg yolk, then pan-fry to make *minari-chodae*.
- Slice the cod fillet thinly, season with salt, then coat with flour and beaten eggs, in that order, to pan-fry.

Cutting the ingredients into the golpae shape
- Make sure the crepes, water celery skewers, cod fritters and soaked shiitake mushrooms are cut to fit the bowl of the *sinseollo*, then into the same width to make small rectangular (*golpae*) shapes.
- Slice the shank, Korean radish, beef tripe and lung thinly, then into the same rectangular shapes.
- Chop the octopuses' legs to a length that will fit the sinseollo bowl and tie a few pieces together with thin legs.

Placing the ingredients in the sinseollo
- Season some of the shank and radish slices with the sauce and soup ingredients, and arrange them flat on the bottom of the *sinseollo* bowl. Place each group of *golpae*-shaped ingredients neatly over the shank and radish slices, followed by the sliced abalones and sea cucumber. Be mindful of the colour presentation for a balanced look. Top the dish with the meatballs, ginkgo nuts and octopus.
- Pour the broth into the bowl and bring it to a boil, allowing the flavours of the various ingredients to blend. Season with *cheongjang* (light soy sauce) and salt to taste.
- Carefully place cooked rice in the centre of a serving bowl, then arrange the ingredients around the rice, ensuring the shapes remain intact. Pour the hot broth over the assembled ingredients.

WINTER

개성무찜
Gaeseong-mu-jjim
Gaeseong braised beef, pork and chicken

Gaeseong's autumn/winter radish was famous for its firm texture and savory flavour, making it worthy of being served on the king's table. *Gaeseong-mu-jjim* is a typical braised dish from the region where beef, chicken, pork, radish and mushrooms are simmered together with various spices during the season when radishes taste best. In the late Goryeo dynasty, the technique of using different types of meat in a single dish emerged, influenced by Mongolian culture and advances in slaughtering methods. This blending of meats is a hallmark of Gaeseong cuisine.

Ingredients
½ Korean radish
500 g (1 lb 1⅝ oz) beef finger meat
500 g (1 lb 1⅝ oz) pork belly
500 g (1 lb 1⅝ oz) chicken thighs
7 *doraji* (bellflower roots)
ginkgo and pine nuts

Marinade
8 tbsps soy sauce
240 ml (1 cup) Korean pear juice
5 tbsps water
3 tbsps *mirin*
3 tbsps *cheongju* (Korean rice wine)
3 tbsps sugar
2 tbsps sesame oil
2 tbsps grated onions
2 tbsps minced spring onion (scallion)
1 tbsp crushed garlic
black pepper

Method
- Cut the radish into 4 cm (1½ in.) long rounds, then slice them into thick sticks (about the size of a finger) and sprinkle with flour.
- Cut the beef finger meat, pork belly and chicken thighs into bite-sized pieces.
- Peel the *doraji* (bellflower roots) and cut into 3 cm (1¼ in.) long strips.
- Mix the marinade ingredients to make a sauce for the steamed radish.
- Add a little bit of sauce to the radish and the *doraji*, and mix well.
- Place the beef finger meat and pork belly in a heavy-bottomed pot, add some water and the sauce, and bring to a boil. Once brought to a boil, add the radish and cook over a low heat.
- Season the chicken thighs with salt and pepper, then cut them to the appropriate size, and stir-fry until half cooked.
- Cook the beef finger meat and pork belly until the marinade permeates, then add the chicken thighs and bring to a simmer.

WINTER

송도식혜
Songdo-sikhye
Sweet rice drink with fruits

Sikhye is a traditional sweet drink made by fermenting cooked rice in malt water, then sweetening and boiling it before serving chilled. A record of *sikhye* from Songdo (the old name of Gaeseong) appears in *Somunsaseol* (*A Book of Practical Knowledge and Skills*). It contains detailed instructions on how to make it tastier than the *sikhye* eaten in Hanyang. The text mentions, 'If you put a whole *yuja* (yuzu) in cooked rice, it makes the flavour more fragrant, the rice grains all intact, the colour milky white, and the taste sweeter.' At Onjium, a variation of *sikhye* is offered, which combines the flavours of *yuja* with fruits like Korean pear and apple, added to a well-fermented *sikhye*.

Ingredients
960 ml (4 cups) malt
2.5 L (2½ qts) water
750 g (5 cups) cooked rice
200 g (1 cup) sugar
1 Korean pear
1 apple
ginger
yuja (yuzu) zest
pine nuts

Method
- Soak the malt in 1200 ml (5 cups) of water for 30 minutes and massage the malt to extract a milky white liquid.
- Pour the malt water through a sieve to strain the liquid. Pour the remaining water into the filtered residue and massage it several times. Strain it again, ensuring that the second batch of water is separated from the first batch.
- Place the cooked rice in a rice cooker pot, pour the first batch of malt water over the rice, and spread the grains evenly. Add 100 g (½ cup) of sugar, cover with a lid, and set the rice cooker on 'warm' for about 5 hours.
- When the rice grains float to the top, pour the mixture into a pot, add the second batch of liquid and the remaining sugar, and boil for about 30 minutes. Remove the froth as it forms. Cool the drink in the refrigerator.
- Peel the pear and apple, then cut them into julienne strips. Slice the ginger and *yuja* (yuzu) zest into julienne strips.
- Place the strips of pear, apple, ginger and *yuja* in a bowl. Pour the chilled *sikhye* over the top and garnish with pine nuts before serving.

다식
Dasik
Pressed tea confection

During the Goryeo era, the custom of drinking tea became widespread and evolved alongside *yumil-gwa*, a traditional confectionery. Among the accompanying tea treats was *dasik*, a type of pressed sweet that highlights the natural colours and flavours of its ingredients. *Dasik* comes in a variety of forms, such as white flour *dasik*, yellow pine pollen *dasik*, black sesame *dasik*, and red *omija* (magnolia berry) *dasik*. Of these, black sesame *dasik* requires the most effort, celebrated for its rich, nutty flavor and nutritional value. Onjium was inspired by the peony prints found in the royal court and created is own *dasik* mould. Onjium's black sesame *dasik* and *jinmal* (wheat flour) *dasik* carry the symbolic wishes of long life, happiness, good health and wellbeing – expressed through the elegance of the peony pattern.

Black sesame dasik

1 kg (2 lb 4 oz) roasted black sesame seed powder
500 g (1 lb 1⅝ oz) honey
salt

Method
- Add salt to the black sesame seed powder, mix well. Place the mixture in a bowl with the honey, cover with plastic wrap, and steam in a preheated steamer for 30 to 40 minutes.
- When the mixture appears glossy, remove from the steamer and pound with a pestle.
- Continue pounding until the colour deepens and the mixture clumps together easily.
- Press the mixture firmly into a *dasik* mould, then carefully remove and cut into bite-sized pieces.

Jinmal dasik

120 g (1 cup) flour
3 tbsps honey

Method
- Sift the flour through a fine sieve, then pan-fry it over a low heat until golden brown.
- Add the honey to the flour, knead thoroughly until smooth, and press firmly into a *dasik* mould.
- Cut into bite-sized pieces.

The Roots and Wings of Korean Food: Onjium's Goryeo Cuisine

Jeong Hye Gyeong
Director of Onjium Food Studio

Korean cuisine is experiencing a global surge in popularity, with high demand in gastronomic capitals from Paris and London to Madrid and New York. As Korean culture continues to captivate the world, it is increasingly evident that our food is poised to become its next leading force. A new era for Korean cuisine has clearly begun.

As we enter this new era, we look back and ask: where do the true roots of Korean cuisine lie? Until now, we have often sought answers in the food of the Joseon dynasty. Joseon-era cuisine is, without question, refined and remarkable. But the time has come to move beyond its boundaries and explore deeper archetypes of traditional Korean food. To transcend Joseon is to turn to ancient history – reaching further back to uncover the foundational layers of our culinary heritage.

Onjium has long been dedicated to reviving traditional culture in forms that feel both renewed and undiminished for the present day. Until now, that work has largely drawn from the legacy of the Joseon dynasty. But Onjium is now turning further back – to the origins of Korean cuisine – by focusing on the extraordinary cultural brilliance of the Goryeo era and its food. The aim is to rediscover the foundations of Korean culinary heritage in the cuisine that flourished in the kingdom's capital, Gaeseong, and was enjoyed by its culturally sophisticated and economically vibrant people.

Goryeo Food, the Root of Korean Cuisine

Korean cuisine has evolved over thousands of years, and its earliest archetypes can be found not in Joseon, but in the food of the preceding Goryeo dynasty. One could argue that the true brilliance of Goryeo culture was most vividly expressed through its cuisine. Yet, discussions of Goryeo culture today rarely acknowledge its culinary achievements. Much of the existing research on traditional Korean food remains centred on the better-documented Joseon period, while the rich and inventive food culture of Goryeo remains largely unexplored. The scarcity of surviving material makes the study of Goryeo cuisine especially challenging – but it is precisely this gap that inspires us to journey into the Goryeo era, in search of new meaning and forgotten flavours.

Goryeo, Land of Ingenuity in International Relations

Goryeo stands as one of the most inspired and resilient kingdoms in Korean history. Spanning nearly 500 years, it endured through an era marked by intense turbulence across East Asia. More than a millennium ago, Goryeo ushered in a period that would ultimately lend modern Korea its very name. Over five centuries, the kingdom preserved its noble lineages, navigated complex relations with powers such as the Khitans, Jurchens and Mongols, and strategically strengthened ties with Japan. Though frequently tested by invasions and internal military uprisings, Goryeo remained committed to cultural exchange, both domestically and abroad. It was this unrelenting openness – even in the face of upheaval – that nourished the emergence of a uniquely sophisticated Goryeo cuisine.

Reciprocal culinary influence connected Goryeo to its surrounding countries. More specifically, relations with the Song dynasty flourished during the century spanning the reign of King Munjong to that of King Injong, with a particular emphasis on the dealing of foodstuffs via merchant ships, due to the Song dynasty's preeminence in maritime trade. Black pepper and sugar – luxury items sought after in high class society during the mid-Goryeo era – entered the kingdom from Song, as did the prevalence of noodle consumption. Meanwhile, the people of Song imported Goryeo celadon – being fond of its stunning jade-green shade – and also responded favourably to the kingdom's mother-of-pearl lacquerwork.

The Yuan dynasty was likewise a frequent partner in culinary exchange. The *History of Goryeo (Goryeosa)* shows that the empress dowager of Yuan sent 40 sheep in commemoration of the royal natal day in the 23rd year of King Chungnyeol's reign. Whereas the people of Goryeo had not previously eaten lamb due to their environment being unconducive to sheep farming, trade relations with Yuan encouraged lamb consumption to the point that the meat began to be included in food for ancestral memorial rites (*jesa*). Having suffered from war-induced famine, Goryeo imported approximately 2.9 million kilograms (6.4 million pounds) of rice from Yuan in the 15th year of King Wonjong's reign and also had 14.4 million kilograms (32 million pounds) of Jiangnan rice delivered on 47 ships in the 17th year of King Chungnyeol's reign. This was the first instance of rice importation in Korean history.

The Goryeo song 'Dumpling Store' (*Ssanghwajeom*) provides yet another example of the lively international relations during this period. As we see in the line, 'I went to the dumpling store to buy some dumplings when the *hoehoeabi* caught hold of my wrist', the *ssanghwajeom* of the song's title proves to be a dumpling store run by a *hoehoeabi*, a term which likely refers to a Uyghur Muslim individual. There was a sizeable population of foreigners living in Gaeseong during the reign of King Chungnyeol when these songs were written, as Goryeo was engaged in a bustling exchange with the Islamic world by way of the Yuan dynasty. Goryeo had become a multicultural society of sorts, so that the markets of Gaeseong offered food from more than a few different countries.

Goryeo, Land of Tea
Goryeo was a land of tea. Tea culture developed in leaps and bounds during the Three Kingdoms (*Samguk*) and Goryeo periods and spread its influence north to Khitan and south to Japan, although the prestige of Goryeo tea culture waned in the Joseon era and was reduced to a mere shadow of its former self. Tea came to the peninsula via China in the mid-7th century during the reign of Shilla's Queen Seondeok and began to be cultivated in earnest from the early 9th century onwards. Daeryeom, envoy to the Tang dynasty, is said to have brought back the seeds of the tea plant and scattered them on Jiri Mountain, paving the way for tea consumption. Tea belonged among the indispensable Buddhist offerings and, from the mid-7th century onwards, was considered as necessary to the everyday lives of the nobility as it was in the official ceremonies of the monarchy and the temples. The demand for tea grew much greater in the Goryeo period than it had been during the Three Kingdoms (*Samguk*) era, prompting the installation and operation of a government tea room (*dabang*) in charge of establishing and implementing overall policy concerning the tea required for official ceremonies in a royal and national capacity. The people of Goryeo made a great many tea confections (*dasik*), which led to the simultaneous development of the moulds needed to produce them. Tea confections (*dasik*) survived throughout the Joseon dynasty and remain to this day an important type of traditional Korean confectionery (*hangwa*). We also have fragmentary records of tea confection (*dasik*) rituals.

Goryeo, Land of Drink
For the entirety of their history, our people have delighted in drinking and revelry. Rites to heaven (*jecheon*) such as the yeonggo of Buyeo, the dongmaeng of Goguryeo, and the mucheon of Dongye combined shamanistic meaning with dancing and singing in groups. The Three Kingdoms' (*Samguk*) proficiency in the brewery was such that Chinese records from the period often mention our alcohol and our technique of brewing from a sorghum barley malt spread all the way to Japan. In the Goryeo era, old methods of brewing rice wine developed even further; refined rice wine (*cheongju*), coarse liquor (*takju*), and hard liquor (*soju*) – currently the most representative of Korean alcoholic beverages – came about in the late Goryeo period thanks to the adoption of distillation processes. At the time, alcohol was either grain- or fruit-based and the hard liquor (*soju*) was distilled rather than diluted as it is today. During the reign of King Chungnyeol, hard liquor entered Goryeo from the Islamic world via the Yuan dynasty; it was called *arrak* in Arabic and *alki* in the Manchu language, which turned into the term *arangju* in the North Pyeongan area and *arakju* in Gaeseong.

We find meticulous accounts of Goryeo drinking culture in not only the *Illustrated Account of the Embassy to Goryeo in the Xuanhe Era* (*Xuanhe Fengshi Gaoli Tujing*) written by a Song dynasty envoy during the early Goryeo period but also the *Essentials of Goryeo History* (*Goryeosajeoryo*) and the *History of Goryeo* (*Goryeosa*). According to these records, the people of Goryeo tended to brew their rice wine out of non-glutinous rice, with coarse liquor (*takju*) more often than not serving as the commoner's drink. The monarchy used refined rice wine (*cheongju*) during national ceremonies, in the royal shrine and royal fields, and for rituals carried out by the king himself on behalf of the state or the royal shrine in the first month of each of the four seasons and at the end of the year. Refined rice wine made according to procedure (*beopju*) fulfilled ceremonial purposes for the state or the royal family in functions during which the official in charge of the royal shrine would act as a proxy. Traditional rice wine (*yakju*) was the alcohol of choice for the Buddhist Festival of the Eight Vows (*palgwanhoe*). Drinking culture within the Goryeo monarchy also shaped the development of gold and silver drinking vessels.

The Beautiful and Decorative Tableware of Goryeo
There was considerable variety in the dishes and vessels used during the Goryeo period, which spanned brassware, lacquerware, goldenware and silverware, golden and silver ceramics, bronzeware and Goryeo celadon. Goryeo celadon, in particular, rose to the height of its development in the mid- Goryeo era (the early 13th century) before and after the reign of King Gojong and came to epitomize the kingdom as a whole. It survives today as a major component of our cultural heritage and an exemplar of an intricate and distinctly Korean aesthetic. When they were made, however, the majority of Goryeo celadon served as the bottles, cups, rice bowls, soup bowls and plates which the people of the kingdom used from day to day. Indeed, Goryeo celadon was common tableware. What sort of food graced such elegant and lovely dishes?

In the 12th and 13th centuries, Goryeo's ceramic artistry reached remarkable heights, with celadon pieces often inscribed with poetic lines, serving as vessels for alcohol at the table. These intricate works were not just functional but deeply symbolic, reflecting the cultural importance placed on dining and the rituals surrounding it. In the 14th century, celadon evolved further, with pieces inscribed with the names of government offices responsible for overseeing the storage and distribution of alcohol. One notable example of this is the prunus vases (*maebyeong*), which were allocated to government offices managing the palace's food and drink, including those overseeing the royal finances, storehouses and the royal table itself.

In 2007, the National Research Institute of Maritime Cultural Heritage excavated a Goryeo-era ship off the coast of Dae Island located in the Taean area of South Chungcheong Province. Onboard, they uncovered an astonishing 27,000 pieces of celadon. Wooden tags attached to or placed beside the cargo revealed that the ship had been a transport vessel, ferrying porcelain from Gangjin in South Jeolla Province to Gaeseong for delivery to members of the nobility and low-ranking military officers. Among the thousands of celadon artefacts recovered from the seabed, one type stood out in particular: the celadon monk's bowl (*baru*). A *baru* is a bowl traditionally used in Buddhist temples for offerings or collecting daily alms. Remarkably, over 40 celadon monk's bowls were found on the Taean ship, providing compelling evidence of both the widespread distribution of Buddhist ritual objects and the close ties between Goryeo's religious culture and its ceramic production.

Right:
Goryeo celadon bowl

Pages 230–31:
Goryeo stone ewers and bronze *kundika* (water bottle)

The Ma Island Shipwreck and the Lives of the People of Goryeo

The discovery of several shipwrecks has provided unspoiled physical evidence of the dietary habits and preferences of the people of Goryeo-era Gaeseong. These wrecked ships, which lay undisturbed beneath the sea for nearly a thousand years, were cargo vessels that supplied goods via the west coast maritime routes during the Goryeo period. Their contents reveal that the people of Gaeseong sourced diverse provisions from across the peninsula and maintained a richly varied diet. The waters surrounding Ma Island (in the Geunheung area of South Chungcheong Province) yielded the Mado 1 in 2009, the Mado 2 in 2010 and the Mado 3 in 2011. The wealth of artefacts recovered from these ships has earned them the nickname 'Gaeseong under the sea'.

In addition to grain products such as hulled and unhulled rice, soybeans, millet and buckwheat, the Mado 1 ship carried a broad range of salted seafood (*jeotgal*), offering a rich trove of insight into the dietary habits of the Goryeo period. The earthenware jars containing *jeotgal* alone numbered nearly 30, each accompanied by wooden tags identifying their contents – salted crab, mackerel and other fish, as well as various fermented foods including soybean blocks and yeast. *Jeotgal* was a beloved side dish, found not only on the modest tables of commoners but also among the ceremonial spreads of the royal court.

Among the most extraordinary findings from the Mado 2 shipwreck was a pair of celadon prunus vases (*maebyeong*) accompanied by bamboo labels. Exceptional even among their exquisitely crafted peers, these prunus vases represent a particular point of pride in Korea's cultural heritage. Two previously unknown facts emerged upon deciphering the bamboo labels. First, the people of Goryeo referred to these celadon prunus vases as kegs (*jun*). Second, and even more surprisingly, they were used for the everyday storage of sesame oil and honey. Until this discovery, scholars had assumed that prunus vases were intended for water or flowers, making their use for storing oil and honey both unexpected and intriguing. The people of Gaeseong valued sesame oil and honey enough to have them transported all the way from Jeolla Province in these prized vessels.

The earthenware discovered on the Mado 3 contained a range of ingredients and fermented foods. Accompanying wooden tags provided detailed information – not only about the food itself but also the place of origin, sender, recipient, type and quantity of each item. Thanks to this manifest, we now know that the Mado 3 carried barley, abalone, fermented abalone, mussels, dried mussels, fermented mussel, shark meat, fish oil and even jerk pheasant.

The Seasonal Customs of Goryeo

Unlike the Confucian formalities of the Joseon dynasty, the seasonal customs of Goryeo were a combination of Buddhist rites led by the ruling royalty and the Confucian practices of the monarchy. The former included the Lotus Lantern Festival (*yeondeunghoe*) in February, Buddha's Birthday on 9 April, the Ullambana Ceremony (*uranbunjae*) on 15 July and the Festival of the Eight Vows (*palgwanhoe*) in November. Thanks to widespread assimilation, these Buddhist seasonal customs succeeded in further enriching the culinary culture of Goryeo. In his poem entitled *Dano*, Lee Saek depicts the Goryeo Dano Festival (a commemoration of the fifth day of the fifth month in the Korean lunar calendar) as well as the merrymaking of the 15 June Festival (*yuduhoe*), complete with jade goblets and bamboo leaf wine (*jugyeopcheong*). One seasonal Goryeo custom with a modern-day counterpart was New Year's Eve (*suse*), which involved sending out the old year and ushering in the new by setting off fireworks, making pastilles for plague prevention (*byeogondan hwanyak*), and drawing good luck talismans (*bujeok*).

Gaeseong Food, the Wings of Korean Cuisine

There is a historical background to the important role that Gaeseong food has come to play in the formulation of Korean cuisine – namely, that of the ancient capital of 500 years and its flavours and traditions. Food essentially matures for the purpose of keeping wealthy palates entertained, making it difficult for a sophisticated cuisine to emerge in regions harried by the burden of mere survival. As the capital of Goryeo, Gaeseong saw the influx and merger of diverse aspects of foreign culture unfold on the most ideal terms and benefitted from the ensuing development of a unique culinary culture.

Upon the founding of the Joseon dynasty, Gaeseong lost its political influence and wholly devoted itself to commerce instead, giving rise to the term 'Gaeseong merchant'. Throughout the Joseon era, Gaeseong guarded its traditions as if it were an island nation. The foremost among those traditions was the city's food. Gaeseong's brand of mild (*seumseum*) flavour – neither salty nor spicy – has remained intact, providing Korean cuisine with a crucial characteristic of its own. For this reason, Gaeseong food is said to have true character (the Korean name for Gaeseong and the Korean word for 'character/personality' are spelled and pronounced the same way), embodying the best values of beauty and culture.

The Flavours of Gaeseong Food

Our modern-day diet abounds with meat, sugar and salt. We are constantly overeating. Where do we turn to discover the genuine flavours of Korean cuisine? The key lies in the food of Gaeseong and the history and culture of Goryeo within it.

The Free-Spirited Flavours of an International City

Goryeo fostered diplomatic and cultural relations with the Jurchens, Khitans, the Song and the Yuan. Its capital, Gaeseong, flourished as an international hub, regularly visited by foreign envoys and continuously engaged in global exchange. In the Goryeo song 'Dumpling Store' (*Ssanghwajeom*), the *hoehoeabi* shopkeeper is identified as a Muslim – reflecting the diversity of the city. Ox bone soup (*seolleongtang*) was influenced by Yuan cuisine. Distilled spirits arrived from Persia, while sugar and black pepper were introduced via the Yuan. These currents of international culinary exchange infused Gaeseong with a multicultural, free-spirited palette of flavours.

The Flavours of Goryeo's Monarchy Come to Life

The nearly 500 years Gaeseong served as the capital of Goryeo endowed it with the solid foundation needed to forge a remarkable legacy of cultural achievement. History and culture are the wellsprings of a region's cuisine. As the heart of Goryeo royalty and nobility, Gaeseong became the cradle of the kingdom's most exquisite culinary creations, home to both Goryeo celadon and a singular cultural heritage. The history of Goryeo's monarchy found new life in the flavours of Gaeseong cuisine.

The Flavours of Buddhism

Buddhism was the predominant religion of Goryeo, and its influence permeated the kingdom's culinary culture. As meat consumption declined, vegetarian diets and a sophisticated tea culture flourished. Elaborate tea spreads evolved alongside the tea rituals themselves, featuring oil-and-honey pastries (*yumilgwa*) and refined confections (*dasik*) that exemplified elegance and delicacy. Certain temples in the capital even produced tofu and brewed alcohol, further contributing to the kingdom's diverse culinary landscape.

The Rich Flavours of the Gaeseong Merchants

A flourishing culinary culture is rooted in economic prosperity. Even in the Joseon era, it was often the financially secure upper middle-class families – not impoverished noble households – who advanced the sophistication of Korean cuisine. Wealth enables refinement, and in Gaeseong, it was the city's prosperous merchant class that elevated its culinary traditions. Their accumulated riches allowed Gaeseong's food culture to thrive, innovate and attain new levels of excellence.

The Flavours of Freedom

While Joseon society was strictly governed by Confucian ideals, shaping its table manners and dietary habits, Goryeo presented a contrasting landscape. The Goryeo era, influenced by its nobles and free-spirited military officers, embraced a more indulgent and flexible approach to food. This freedom is distinctly reflected in the diverse culinary culture of the time.

The Flavours Crafted from the Correspondence of Diverse Ingredients

Surrounded by the ocean, mountain ranges and expansive plains, Gaeseong had access to the bounties of both land and sea. Its tables were graced with a rich variety of ingredients, including meats, seafood, grains and *sannamul* (wild greens). The culinary culture of Gaeseong was, therefore, a reflection of the abundance of the land, which offered a diverse and plentiful array of ingredients to craft its exceptional flavours.

The Savoury Flavours of Bountiful Seafood and Salted Seafood (Jeotgal)

With its proximity to the ocean, Gaeseong was blessed with an abundance of seafood. A particularly prominent ingredient was the *saeujeot* (fermented prawn/shrimp), sourced from the plentiful catches in the western sea, which added a deep savoury flavour to Gaeseong's culinary foundation. These *saeujeot* were also the ideal seasoning for pork, creating a distinctive taste profile that set Gaeseong's pork dishes apart from those of other regions.

The Happy Medium – Neither Salty, Nor Bland

Contemporary trends in Korean cuisine often favour extremes – intense spiciness, saltiness, or sweetness. The once-dominant spice craze has gradually given way to a salty-sweet obsession. While these bold flavours offer a dangerously addictive allure, they tend to overwhelm the subtle, inherent tastes of our traditional dishes. Such extremes dull our palates, leaving us constantly chasing stronger sensations to satisfy increasingly desensitized taste buds. Despite Korea's modest size, the country has long been marked by distinct regional flavour profiles – spicier, saltier fare in the south, and milder, soup-based dishes in the north. Situated at the midpoint of the peninsula, Gaeseong not only held geographical and political significance as the Goryeo capital but also developed a culinary style that struck a harmonious balance: neither overly salty nor bland. This moderation became a hallmark of Gaeseong's refined and temperate taste.

The Gaeseong Food of Today

While there are all too regrettably parts of the cuisine gradually fading from our collective knowledge, the origins of Gaeseong food do surface in the dishes that we appreciate today.

Familiarizing ourselves with representative examples of Gaeseong food will provide us with a straight path forwards to truly understanding Korean cuisine.

Joraengitteok-guk (Joraengi Rice Cakes in Clear Beef Soup)
On New Year's Day, the people of Gaeseong ate a distinctively shaped rice cake soup. There are multiple theories as to the origins of pinched rice cakes (*joraengitteok*). One tells of the people of Gaeseong making the rice cakes as though they were throttling Lee Seonggye (King Taejo of the Joseon dynasty) out of hatred for his having brought about the downfall of Goryeo. Another says that the rice cakes were meant to look like the bottle gourds (*jorongbak*) that would drive away evil spirits if you drummed on them. Yet others maintain that the rice cakes symbolize good luck for the year due to their resemblance to silkworm cocoons or that the pinched rice cake soup (*joraengitteok-guk*) brings to mind a string of brass coins (*yeopjeon*) and is therefore consumed on New Year's morning as a wish for the household coffers to overflow. With its many origin stories, pinched rice cake soup (*joraengitteok-guk*) is the quintessential example of Gaeseong food.

Gaeseong-bo-kimchi (Gaeseong Wrapped Kimchi)
A Gaeseong Delicacy
The Gaeseong wrapped *kimchi* (*gaeseong-bo-kimchi*) emerged at the pinnacle of Gaeseong's blooming culinary culture. More than just a side dish, this *kimchi* constitutes an individual dish in its own right and is considered the most beautiful type of *kimchi* to come from the nation that originated this fare. Shredded green onions, garlic, ginger and red peppers are added to a cabbage leaf; the cabbage leaf is then used to wrap and ferment a stuffing of Asian pear, chestnuts, Korean dates (*jujubes*) and seafood such as octopus, abalone and oysters. Extravagant and ostentatious, the comely presentation and refined flavours of wrapped *kimchi* (*bo-kimchi*) were a credit even to the most lavish banquet table.

From Sanghwa (Dumplings of Song) to Gaeseongpyeonsu (Square Dumplings)

Dumplings are a representative North Korean dish, but the dumplings of Gaeseong by no means fall behind their Pyeongyang counterparts. Gaeseong dumplings are known for being adorable little morsels. They also encompass the square dumpling (*pyeonsu*), a form seldom if ever seen in other regions. The square dumpling is a summer dish made of vegetable and meat stuffing and a thinly rolled flour wrapper stuck together by each of its four corners, steamed or boiled before being consumed cold with a vinegar-laced soy sauce dip. The stuffing generally consists of stir-fried and seasoned beef mixed with boiled mung bean sprouts and tender summer squash that has been julienned, parboiled and drained of liquid.

Gaeseong-jangttaengi (Gaeseong Pancake)
The Comfort Food of Gaeseong

Unlike similar dishes from other regions, Gaeseong pancakes (*gaeseong-jangttaengi*) include ground meat and undergo a fermentation process that gives them a rich flavour. The name suggests little more than a sort of fried pancake (*buchimgae*) with bean paste added into the batter, but the dish boasts a long history dating back to the records of the 1600s. Those from Gaeseong remember it as their comfort food, emblematic of the caring sensibilities of the city's people.

Honghaesam (Red Sea Cucumber Stuffed Omelette)
The Ceremonial Food of Gaeseong

The ingredients for this dish consist of sea cucumbers and mussels from off the coast of Hwanghae Province, coveted even by the Chinese. The concoction was unique enough to earn itself a special place at ceremonial feasts and came to be considered the Gaeseong standard for a fine spread. Red sea cucumbers and mussels (*honghaesam*) were often prepared for post-wedding greeting ceremonies (*pyebaek*) and wedding banquets. Because the black sea cucumbers inside the yellow egg wrap stood for the man and the red mussels inside the white egg wrap stood for the woman, both were placed on a single plate to wish for a harmonious marriage. Dried mussels and dried sea cucumbers require the intensive labour of repeated steaming and drying, but reward the palate with a corresponding degree of rich flavour.

Oi-seon (Stuffed Cucumber Bites)
A Gaeseong Beauty

Stuffed cucumber bites (*oi-seon*) are a Gaeseong specialty, traditionally presented in combination with plenty of broth to the point that the dish resembles a soup. In the *Book of Agriculture (Nongjeonghoeyo)* published in 1830, it appears as a pressed cucumber dish (*hwanggwaranbeop*) accompanied by the following instructions: 'First peel an old cucumber, split it down the middle in three different directions, and scrape out some of the insides. Separately, rinse your beef several times until the water no longer runs bloody. Add in the ingredients and pound them until minced, then add a little flour and stuff the inside of the cucumber to capacity. Place and boil the stuffed cucumber in water well-seasoned with soy sauce before eating.' The displaced residents of Gaeseong had particularly vivid and persistent memories of this dish.

Moyakgwa (Square Flaky Pastry with Honey) and Gaeseong ju-ak (Rice Cakes a la Gaeseong)
The Desserts of Gaeseong

Honey pastries (*yakgwa*) are a representative fried honey cake (*gwajul*) made with flour, honey and oil. A type of oil-and-honey pastry (*yumil-gwa*), they were often included in Buddhist ceremonies and consumed by the royal family during the Goryeo period, delectable and recognizable enough to be well-known even as far as China. Gaeseong, in particular, made a square-shaped rendition of this pastry (*moyakgwa*) for use during feasts and ancestral memorial rites (*jesa*).

Rice cakes a la Gaeseong (*gaeseong ju-ak*) – also called *umegi* – are a type of traditional Korean confectionery (*hangwa*) specific to Gaeseong. Glutinous rice flour and wheat flour are mixed together and fermented with unrefined rice wine (*makgeolli*), then fried and coated in honey and powdered cinnamon (*jipcheong*) so as to prevent the doughnuts from hardening. As the saying, 'You can't have a feast without *umegi*' indicates, the people of Gaeseong relished this treat during meals as well as for dessert.

Onjium's Offering of Gaeseong Flavours

'The greatest of flavours are ever mild and modest.'
The Book of Han (Hanshu)

The more superior the flavour, the more unerringly it is mild and modest.

Potent flavours dazzle at first bite, but soon tire out the tongue, while those which are mild and modest infuse the mouth at leisure and long hold the palate captive to their graces.

True to its roots – nearly 500 years in the making as the capital of the Goryeo dynasty – Gaeseong's culinary tradition is deeply anchored in the refined gastronomic culture cultivated by Goryeo royalty and nobility: in short, the distinction and splendour of palace cuisine. This aristocratic legacy coexisted with a rich tapestry of culinary influences: the practical and expansive food culture shaped by trade and diplomatic exchange; the abundance and generosity of the merchant class, nourished by their considerable wealth; the vegetarian diet and sophisticated tea and confectionery culture – featuring tea and oil-and-honey pastries (*yumil-gwa*) – fostered by Buddhism as the national religion; and the humble, grounded fare of the common people, rooted in the natural resources of field, mountain, river and sea.

In comparison to the rugged mountain ranges and bitter winters encircling the other northern areas of the peninsula, Gaeseong abounded in the delicacies of the fields and mountains and the blessings of the sea, enjoying a profusion of ingredients, including meat, grain, seafood, *sannamul* (wild greens) and fruit. The city accordingly threw itself wholeheartedly into the production of preparing and consuming food that called for a diverse and well-balanced range of ingredients and exacting care taken at every turn of the process. The citizens of Gaeseong were a people with a singular insistence on embellishing their food even when they refrained from dressing in sumptuous clothing or decking their households in trimmings. They took great pains preparing their meals as they gathered the finest ingredients, sliced them to shapely precision, and controlled the heat with meticulous restraint – which, combined with the sophisticated skill it took to select corresponding tableware, dish up an elegant service, and top everything off with colourful garnishes, birthed the inimitable palate and aesthetics of 'Gaeseong cuisine'.

In a word, Gaeseong cuisine entails 'an unskewed flavour'. We might call this flavour fond and mellow. Reassuring. Understated. Lightly salted, allowed hours and hours to stew. Instead of bombarding the taste buds, it uses delicate seasoning to bring out the utmost from the essence of the ingredients themselves. It is rich and hearty yet mild and modest, the end result of various meats and vegetables simmering together over time. Moreover, it also features the charm inherent to fermentation, the greatest of savoury tastes.

We intend to revive the distinctive 'mildness' of Gaeseong cuisine by taking the foundation of its flavour – passed down to us over the ages and encapsulated within our appetites – and arraying it with the warmth of Onjium's own attempt at reinterpretation; Onjium's sifting of Gaeseong flavours, Onjium's offering of Gaeseong flavours.

Onjium's Alcoholic Beverages

The tastes and flavours of Korean liquors can make exquisite pairings for Korean dishes. The following ten kinds of traditional alcoholic drinks should still be enjoyed today. These alcoholic beverages are brewed by artisans.

Page 235:
Preparation for *yeolguja-tang*

Page 236–37:
White porcelain Korean alcoholic beverage bottles and cups by contemporary artists

1 **Omi Rose**
Made from eco-friendly berries called *omija* ('five flavours') produced by a traditional brewing method in Mungyeong, Gyeongsangbuk-do Province, Omi Rose is a sparkling wine that goes well with Korean dishes. When served as an aperitif, Omi Rose suits dry appetizers such as *bugak* and *yukpo*. A wine with very fine, long-lasting bubbles, Omi Rose impresses drinkers with its mellow but zippy tang.

2 **Samhaeju**
Handed down from the Goryeo period (918–1392), Samhaeju was served at the royal court and to the nobility. It is such a precious delicacy that its brewing technique was designated as a Intangible Cultural Heritage of Seoul. The Koreans brewed delicate, elegant rice wine with a *nuruk* fermentation starter and named it Samhaeju. Samhaeju is a high-end drink very carefully brewed. It is clear and has an excellent flavour and aroma, well suited to Korean dishes.

3 **Heobeokju**
A specialty of Jeju Island, Heobeokju made with clear water in the clean air of the island is named after the island's traditional earthenware called Heobeok. Heobeokju is a modern-day distilled beverage made by fermenting rye and brown rice. Heobeokju has an alcohol content of 35 per cent and a mellow and clean flavour, and it the perfect drink in winter. It goes well with *domijjim* (steamed sea bream), as well as with grilled meat dishes.

4 **Baekhwaju**
Many different flowers that blossom in each season throughout the year are collected and dried to make Baekhwaju ('one-hundred flowers liquor'). Baekhwaju is a fascinating beverage with outstanding flavour. Full bodied with a sour taste, Baekhwaju goes well with sashimi or *naengchae* (cold salad). Baekhwaju is difficult to come by as it requires so much effort to make.

5 **Cheonggamju**
This liquor is named Cheonggamju, meaning 'clear and sweet wine' for its clearness and sweet taste. Unlike other liquors, Cheonggamju is made by mixing high-quality *cheongju* (Korean rice wine) rather than water. As such, only a small quantity of Cheonggamju can be made at a time. Mild and light, Cheonggamju has a sweet, exceptionally pleasing flavour. It goes well with desserts and tastes best when served cold.

6 **Gyeongju Beopju Special Selection**
This is the highest-end *cheongju*, made with utmost care. It requires carefully selected rice harvested in Korea and polished down to 55 per cent, and then fermented at a low temperature and filtered through a cotton sack in the traditional way. The clear and clean flavour and crisp fruit aroma are characteristic of this brand of *cheongju*, and it is hard to find. It goes well with appetizers such as *mandu* (dumplings), sashimi and *naengchae*.

Onjium's Bugak

Bugak are traditional Korean chips made by deep frying or grilling dried vegetables or seaweed that have been coated with thin glutinous rice paste. *Bugak* is a healthy chewy snack with the taste and nutrition of fresh seasonal ingredients. This selection of beautiful *bugak* offer seasonal tastes and flavours.

1 **Gajuk (Chinese Cedar) Bugak**
Made of *gajuk* (young shoots of Chinese cedar); those with short and stubby stems taste better and more tender. Mix *gochujang*, crushed garlic, sugar and fish sauce with glutinous rice flour. Apply this mixture generously to both sides of the leaves of Chinese cedar, dry in the sun until crispy, and then deep fry.

2 **Bangpung (Wild Parsnip) Bugak**
Steamed *bangpung* (wild parsnip leaves) from Geumodo Island in Jeollanam-do are coated with a thin glutinous rice paste made with parsnip stem broth. Dry until crispy and deep fry right before serving.

3 **Eoran (Roe) Bugak**
Mix grilled and ground croaker roe with glutinous rice paste. Spread the mixture thinly and let it dry. It tastes especially good when deep fried or grilled.

4 **Lotus Root Bugak**
This *bugak* is made from peeled and thinly sliced white lotus roots from Chungju, Chungcheongbuk-do Province, that are washed in water to remove starch, boiled in water, dried until crispy and then deep fried.

5 **Potato Bugak**
Pick potatoes produced in mountainous areas of Gangwon-do Province. Slice the potatoes thinly, wash in water to remove starch, boil in salty water and then dry until crispy. When deep fried, the authentic light and clean flavour of potatoes becomes all the more crispy and delicate.

6 **Genaejang (Snow Crab Offal) Bugak**
Made of thick offal of snow crab, this *bugak* is soft, sticky and thick.

7 **Crab Meat Bugak**
Made of snow crab from Uljin, Gyeongsangbuk-do, this crab meat chip is only made at Onjium. After steaming snow crabs, meat is picked out of the crabs and the shells are used to make stock. Add glutinous rice flour to the stock to make a paste, and then mix the crab meat with the paste. Spread the mixture on a thin, paper-like sheet of *gim* (dried seaweed). Let dry on leather, cut into chip size and dry until very crispy. Deep fry or grill right before serving.

8 **Gim (Dried Seaweed) Bugak**
Dried sheets of seaweed collected on Wando Island, Jeollanam-do Province, in winter are coated with glutinous rice paste made of thick anchovy stock. Deep fry or grill right before serving. The distinct aroma and crispy flavour of *gim* (dried seaweed) goes well with alcoholic beverages.

1

2

3

4

Onjium's Jangajji

Jangajji collectively refers to side dishes made by pickling or marinating fresh seasonal ingredients in soy sauce or *doenjang* (fermented soybean paste) and left to slowly ferment. Salty and savoury, and tastes good when biting, *jangajji* is the best accompaniment to rice as it stimulates the appetite. These *jangajji* are made from ingredients unique to Korea and are matured with the utmost care for a long time.

1 **Choseokjam (Chinese Artichoke) Jangajji**
Chinese artichoke tubers are harvested in winter. Smaller tubers look better and are crunchier. Combine 2 parts soy sauce, 1 part sugar, 2 parts water, 1.4 parts vinegar, a few drops of cooking wine and *soju* (Korean hard liquor), a bit of dried red pepper and black pepper, and bring to boil. Turn off the heat and pour the boiled brine over the tubers. If pickled tubers are too salty, marinate them in pear juice for a little while before serving.

2 **Hamcho (Glasswort) Jangajji**
Glasswort grows in salt marshes and on beaches, making it naturally salty. Parboil glasswort and then marinate in 1 part vinegar, 1 part water and 1 part sugar. It goes well with sashimi.

3 **Green Hot Pepper and Leaves Jangajji**
This *jangajji* is made with green chilli peppers and leaves harvested in late autumn. Combine 1 part traditional Korean soy sauce (*guk-ganjang*), 1 part soy sauce, 2 parts water, 1 part sugar and 1.3 parts vinegar and marinate the chilli peppers and leaves in it. Squeeze the pickled peppers and add sesame oil before serving.

4 **Yuja Citron Doenjang Jangajji**
Carve out the insides of the *yujas* (yuzu), and fill the insides with *doenjang* (fermented soybean paste). Steam the stuffed lemons in the steamer and dry steam citrons outside under the eaves. The shells of the citrons will gradually break down and become mixed with the *doenjang*, releasing a delicate aroma. Slice thinly before serving as an accompaniment to alcohol beverages or grind to make *ssamjang*, a dipping sauce.

5 **Dubu(tofu)jang**
Dubujang has long been consumed at temples. It is fermented bean curd marinated in *doenjang* (fermented soybean paste). Similar to the taste of gentle, thick cheese, *dubujang* can be eaten after being preserved for six months.

6 **Kkorangi (Napa Cabbage Roots) Jangajji**
The root ends of native Korean napa cabbage harvested in late autumn are small and taste delicate and sweet. Salt the roots and marinate in 1 part Joseon *guk-ganjang* (traditional Korean soy sauce), 1 part *jin-ganjang*, 2 parts water, 1 part sugar and 1.3 parts vinegar. Shred and mix with sesame oil, ground sesame and starchy syrup before serving.

7 **Eundallae (Pickled Wild Onion) Jangajji**
Combine 2 parts soy sauce, 1 part sugar, 2 parts water and 1.4 parts vinegar, and add a few drops of cooking wine *soju*, dried pepper and black pepper. Pour it over *eundallae* (pickled wild onion), which is harvested in winter in Injae, Gangwon-do Province. With great flavor and biting taste, *eundallae jangajji* can be also used as sauce for dipping *jeon* (Korean pancake).

8 **Eomnamu Gochujang Jangajji**
Also called *gae-dureup*, *eomnamu* shoots are harvested in Gangwon-do Province most commonly. After maturing in soy sauce, dry the shoots slightly and then marinate in *gochujang*. They last for months. *Eomnamu* and *gochujang* make a great pair.

9 **Danggui (Angelica Root) Gochujang Jangajji**
Danggui has a very penetrating aroma and tastes sweet and bitter. Clean *danggui* thoroughly, dry it slightly and marinate in *gochujang*. It can be eaten after six months.

10 **Pine Mushroom Jangajji**
Use flavourful, tasty mushrooms from Geumgang in Uljin, Gyeongsangbuk-do Province. Combine 2 parts soy sauce, 2 parts water and 1 part sugar, and bring to a boil. Turn off the heat and pour the boiled brine over the mushrooms. Cool and keep in the refrigerator. Slice thinly or shred by hand before serving.

Onjium's Tea

1. Lotus Root Tea
Thoroughly clean white lotus root from Chungju, slice thinly and dry. Bake the dried slices in an oven. It tastes good and smells good.

2. Mugwort Tea
Mugwort grown on the windy riverside in Namyangju County is used. Roast in a pot and dry. Dry a second time in the pot. Mugwort tea helps to treat gastritis and colds and effectively keeps the body warm.

3. Burdock Root (Ueong) Tea
Thoroughly clean burdock roots (*ueong*), slice crosswise, and dry. Roast them in a pot. Burdock root tea tastes mild and is good to drink every day instead of water.

4. Bamboo Shoot (Juksun) Tea
Bamboo shoots (*juksun*) are a vegetable that herald the arrival of spring. Bamboo shoots collected in Damyang are used. Steam only the soft parts of the bamboo shoots and dry before roasting in a pot.

5. Dried Yuja (Yuzu) Citron Tea
Organic *yuja* (yuzu) from Jeju Island is used. Shred the *yuja* after removing the seeds, and then dry on a wicker tray. Roast in a pot.

6. Dried Yeonggyul (Tangerine) Tea
Remove the seeds of Jeju Island *yeonggyul* (tangerine) and shred. Dry the shredded *yeonggyul* and then roast in a pot. *Yeonggyul* is usually preserved as *cheong* (extract), but dried *yeonggyul* makes a very savoury tea with a sour and somewhat bitter taste.

Onjium's Fruit and Vegetable Marmalades

1 Mulberry Marmalade

To make mulberry marmalade, fill a jar with the same amounts of sweet, fresh mulberries and sugar.

2 Kumquat Marmalade

Remove the seeds from the kumquats and mix them with the same amount of sugar. The juice should form after a week. At that time, remove the kumquat solids and mix them at a ratio of 5 parts kumquat solids with 1 part water, 1 part honey, and 1 part sugar. Boil the mixture down in a pot to get the extract. The extract is used as a spread or jam, and the juice is used as a sweetener for tea or cooking.

3 Passion Fruit Extract Marmalade

Mix passion fruit with the same amount of sugar to make an extract. It smells so good, the passion fruit extract can be used for various desserts.

4 Pomegranate Marmalade

Select heavy, bright red pomegranates produced in Goheung and mix with sugar and honey. This makes wonderful warm pomegranate tea or cold pomegranateade with a slice of lemon.

5 Ginger Extract Marmalade

Squeeze grated fresh ginger to get juice. Remove the starch formed on the surface of the juice. Bring the clear juice to a boil. Add unrefined organic sugar and honey to the boiled juice and simmer at a low heat.

6 Yeonggyul (Tangerine) Extract Marmalade

Thinly slice crosswise fresh green Jeju Island tangerines and remove the seeds, and mix with same amount of sugar. This makes a great cup of tea, and can also be used as jam.

7 Yuja (Yuzu) Citron Extract Marmalade

Make four vertical cuts into a *yuja* (yuzu) citron and separate the peel and flesh. Remove the seeds from the flesh and mix the peel and flesh separately in same amount of sugar to mature. Shred the matured peels and use them as sweetener for tea or cooking. The flesh extract is a good ingredient for salad dressing.

About Onjium

Onjium Restaurant originated as a one-table kitchen, serving as a test bed for Food Studio's ongoing research and experiments. In 2017, it relocated to its current location and evolved into the Onjium Restaurant known today. Here, about 20 members of staff are fully responsible for every aspect of the dining experience, from preparing a seasonal course meal in the open kitchen to arranging food on plates, decorating the table, serving dishes and explaining ingredients. They tell stories about the vessels used and their makers, and pair the meal with carefully selected alcoholic beverages. This is not just a restaurant that serves Korean food – it is a curated dining experience in the unique style of Onjium.

The restaurant's seasonal menu, renewed every two months, reflects the belief that the roots of Korean cuisine lie in food that embraces the seasons. Onjium tells its stories through the nuanced flavours of unassuming ingredients, avoiding rare and upscale embellishments. Through temperate refinement infused with elegance, it creates a landscape of Korean flair and flavour that belongs to the here and now.

Onjium aims to preserve the legacy of Korean food with affection and sincerity. By blending tradition with a modern sense of beauty and emphasizing seasonal, healthy ingredients, Onjium crafts tables rich in flavour and cultural heritage. This dedication ensures Korean cuisine evolves while staying true to its roots.

Through its commitment to research, innovation and cultural preservation, Onjium has sparked widespread appreciation for Korean cuisine, both domestically and internationally. Its work fosters pride in Korean heritage and inspires sensitivity to the flavours and traditions that define it. As Onjium continues its journey, it invites others to savour the beauty of its creations and participate in shaping Korean cuisine's future. May this publication mark the next step in Onjium's mission to celebrate and share the rich legacy of Korean food.

Acknowledgments

The Art of Korean Cooking came to life thanks to the passion and dedication of three remarkable individuals – Fiona Bae, Lucas Dietrich and Helen Fanthorpe – to whom we extend our deepest gratitude.

We are also sincerely grateful to those who lay the foundation: Onjium Food Studio (Cho Eun Hee, Sungbae Park, Sim Soo Jeong, Lee Seunglip, Kim Yu Jung, Ye Keon Yun, Kim Esther, Lee Sang Yun, Sara Lee, Song Jaehoon, Sim Seonghyeon), Onjium Planning Department (J. Kathryn Hong, Joanne Bonhee Koo), and STUDIO KIO.

Finally, our heartfelt thanks go to two masters of photography – Bae Bien-U and Koo Bohnchang – whose powerful images have brought depth and richness to this publication.

About the Contributors

Woongchul Park
Born in South Korea and trained in the US, Korea and the UK, Woongchul Park now cooks in London, where he runs restaurant Sollip with his wife Bomee Ki, who is also co-owner and pastry chef. His food is a gentle meeting point between discipline, identity and emotion.

Yun Gyun S. Hong
Hong founded the Arumjigi Culture Keepers Foundation in 2001 with the vision of preserving and contemporizing traditional Korean culture, and served as its Chairperson for 25 years. In 2013, she went on to establish Onjium to support the systematic study of traditional Korean food, clothing and housing culture, as well as the training of artisans. She currently serves as Chair of its Executive Committee.

Jeong Hye Gyeong
Director of the Onjium Food Studio. Initially trained in Western nutrition, Jeong was captivated by the cultural, historical and scientific richness of Korean cuisine.

Hesson Jeong
A culinary culture editor who oversaw the planning, writing and overall production of the two foundational volumes of this book: *Onjium's Cookbook* and *Onjium's Cookbook: Roots and Wings*.

You Hong June
Advisor to the Arumjigi Culture Keepers Foundation and former Head of the Cultural Heritage Administration. An art critic and researcher specializing in Korean art history and cultural heritage.

Photo Credits

By Hee kee Min
pp.7, 12, 15, 16, 19; Spring pp.23–46, 66, 70; Summer pp.77–93; Autumn pp.127–45, 152, 166, 179; Winter pp.183–203, 216, 236–48

By Jongkeun Lee
pp.2, 4, 8–9; Spring pp.49–65, 72–73; Summer pp.95–111; Autumn pp.147–51, 155–65, 169–72; Winter pp.204–15, 219–23, 235

© Bae Bien-U
pp.20, 74, 124, 180

By Koo Bohnchang
pp.69, 174–75, 227, 230–31

Index

Page numbers in *italics* refer to illustrations

A
abalones 26, 40, 44, 47, 50, 62, 76, 128, 164, 167, 184, 208, 214–17, 232
aehobak (Korean summer squash) 44, 47, 98, 206
amberjack 150
amur catfish 154
anchovy sauce
    Korean 62
    salted 184, 187
apple juice 132
apples 164, 167, 220
August-lilies 148

B
ba-kimchi (wrapped *kimchi*) 208
baek-hwaban (bibimbap with white vegetables) 138, *139*
baek-kimchi (white *kimchi*) 208
baek-yukgaejang (mild beef and vegetable soup) 90, *91*
baekgangmil (Korean wheat) 100
bam-jeon (chestnut pancake) 168, *169*
bam-juk (chestnut porridge) 126, *127*
bamboo shoots 26, 30, 48
bangpung 22
bangpung-juk (rice porridge with bangpung leaves) 22, *23*
bean sprouts 196
beans
    black 32
    mung 38, 44, 47, 52, 78, 80, 100, 104, 130, 160, 196
    red 32
beef 24, 38, 44, 47, 64, 78, 80, 86, 90, 94, 96, 108, 134, 144, 148, 190, 208, 210, 214–17, 218
    broth 128, 154, 156, 184, 198, 210
    gravy 26
    marinade 96, 98, 104, 108, 148
    stock 196
beef lung 214–17
beef tripe 214–17
beotgul-naengchae (cold *beotgul* oyster salad) 187, *188*
bidan-meongge (sea pineapple) 187, 208
bo-kimchi 164
bogeo pipyeon (pufferfish skin jelly) 206, *207*
bok-tang (puffer fish soup) 48, *49*
bomnapul bibimbap (*bibimbap* with spring vegetables) 36, *37*
bugak 241
bulgogi sauce 30
burdock (*ueong*) 108, 194
byeongsi (crescent-shaped dumplings) 198

C
cabbage 160, 232
    napa 48, 130, 164, 167, 198
carrots 78, 214
celery, water 94, 130, 154, 164, 167, 214–17
cheollyop-guk (river fish spicy soup) 154, *155*
cheong-ju (Korean rice wine) 170, 173, 218
cheongpo-muk (mung bean starch) 44
cheongyang green pepper 86
chicken 30, 56, 94, 104, 182, 218
    broth 182
    stock 196
chilli powder, Korean 60, 62, 153, 154, 164, 167
chillis 102
chives 104, 154, 160, 210
chodae (Korean water celery skewer) 214–17
cinnamon powder 162, 173
citron peel, Korean 208
clams 54
cod 40, 80, 94, 186, 196, 214–17
coriander (cilantro) salad dressing 206
courgettes (zucchini) 24, 98, 130, 186
crabs 62
    blue (*mujeot*) 54, 60, 158
    snow 130, 186
croaker 80, 102
cucumbers 47, 76, 78, 92
    Korean 48, 96, 102, 104, 150
    sea 44, 47, 48, 52, 156, 214–17, 232

D
daeha jeonbok yukjeup-muchim (prawn/shrimp and abalone with beef gravy) 26, *27*
dan-saewu-mul-hwe (raw sweet prawn/shrimp soup) 76, *77*
dansaeu-mu-jeot (seasoned raw northern prawns) 153
dasik (pressed cookie) 144, 222, *223*
    black sesame 222
dasima myeolchi stock 22, 130, 136, 140
dates, Korean (*jujubes*) 60, 86, 134, 146, 150, 153, 162, 164, 167, 173, 202, 208, 232
    paste 162
deodeok (lance asiabell roots) 50, 182
doenjang (fermented soybean paste) 64, 84, 90, 106, 132, 167
dolryeokkaki 98
domi-jjim (stuffed and steamed red snapper) 38, *39*
dongchimi (white radish water *kimchi*) 92
doraji (bellflower roots) 50, 94, 182, 218
dubu-namul-bap (rice with tofu and vegetables) 58, *59*
dumpling wrapper dough 198
dumplings 232
dwaejigogi jangttaengi (pork pancake) 64

E
eels 88
eggs 28, 38, 44, 47, 52, 88, 92, 94, 156, 158, 196, 198, 206, 214–17
eo-mandu nureumi (fish dumpling drizzled with *nureumi* sauce) 186, *187*
eochae 102
eogyo soondae (*soondae* stuffed in a croaker's air bladder) 80, *81*
eoyuk-kimchi-naengchae (wrapped *kimchi* salad with seafood) 208, *209*
eundallae jangajji (pickled wild onion soy sauce) 36

F
fish porridge 154
fish sauce 187
    Korean 206
flour 186, 198, 222
    buckwheat 98
    glutinous rice 110
    wheat 98, 100, 110

G
Gaeseong juak (deep fried rice cake coated with syrup) 110, *111*, 233
Gaeseong-bo-kimchi (Gaeseong wrapped kimchi) 164–67, *165*, *166*, 232
Gaeseong-jangttaengi (Gaeseong dried pancakes) 64, *65*, *66*, 232
Gaeseong-mu-jjim (Gaeseong braised beef, pork and chicken) 218, *219*
Gaesong yakgwa and *mandu-gwa* (deep fried pastries coated with syrup) 170–73, *171*, *172*

gamcho (liquorice root) 88
ganjang, vinegar (dipping sauce made with soy sauce and vinegar) 102
garlic sauce 76, 187
gasiri 200
gasiri-bokeum (stir-fried *gasiri* seaweed) 200, *201*
ge-gui (soft crab meat pancake) 158, *159*
ge-jjim (steamed crab) 54, *55*
ge-sal-muchim-bap (rice with seasoned crab meat) 60, *61*
gesal-baechu-seon (steamed napa cabbage stuffed with snow crab meat) 130, *131*
ginseng root (*insam*) 104, 146
gochujang, vinegar (dipping sauce made with Korean fermented chilli paste and vinegar) 102
gochujang (red pepper paste) 132, 154
golden mandarin fish 154
gopchang (small cow intestines) 90
gosari (bracken) 90
grapes 86
grapeseed oil 170, 173, 190, 198
gwajul 233

H

haemul jeongol (seafood hot pot) 40, *41*
haesam-jjim (steamed sea cucumber roll with prawns/shrimp) 156, *157*
herring, Pacific 150
hodu-japchae (walnuts with marinated beef and vegetables) 108, *109*
honey 42, 106, 134, 144, 162, 170, 173, 190, 222
honghaesam (sea cucumber and mussel wrap) 52, *53*
honghap-siraegi-mu-bap (rice with dried radish leaves and mussels) 192, *193*
hwalgye-jjim (braised chicken with salted prawns/shrimp) 56, *57*

J

Jangajji 243–44
jangeo-bap (rice with eel) 88, *89*
jat-juk (pine nut porridge) 204, *205*
jeon (Korean fritter) 214–17
jeonbok-jeot and honghap-hae (marinated abalone and mussels) 62, *63*
jeonbok-kkot-jjim (steamed abalone with root vegetables) 50, *51*
jeonbyeong 94
jeoneo (gizzard shad) 132

jeoneo-muchim (*jeoneo* with vegetables) 132, *133*
jidan (Korean egg crepe strips) 214–17
jindallae hwajeon (azalea rice cake) 42, *43*
jinmal dasik (wheat flour *dasik*) 222
jipcheong (spice-infused syrup) 110, 170, 173, 233
jocheong (grain syrup) 110
joraengitteok (rice cakes) 210, 232
ju-ak (*umegi*) 110
juk 146

K

kalguksu (hand-cut noodle) 98
kalssakdugi (hand-cut noodle soup) 98, *99*
kelp, dried (*dasima*) 60, 88, 94, 96, 104, 153, 154, 206, 210
kimchi 98, 164, 167, 208, 232
  juice 164
  napa cabbage 198
kkhae-ganjeong (sesame crunch) 142, *143*
Korean (*guk-ganjang*), soy sauce 28, 30, 36

L

laver 200
Lee Gyubo 54
Lee Saek 58
lemon juice 187, 206
lotus root 140, 194

M

maegjeog-gui (steamed pork belly seasoned and grilled with soybean paste) 106, *107*
maesaengi-jeonbok-tang (abalone and maesangi seaweed soup) 184, *185*
maeseangi seaweed 184
makgeolli (Korean fermented rice alcoholic beverage) 110, 233
malt 220
mandu-gwa 170, 173
marinade 218
marmalades 249
melons, Korean 94
meok-beoseot galbi-jjim-gui 134, *135*
mieum 146
mil-cheonsin (chicken and bellflower root wrap) 94, *95*
mil-ssam (stick roll) 78, *79*
milk 126
minari (Korean watercress) 24, 38, 40, 80, 130, 187, 196
minari-chodae 217

mineo-eochae (brown croaker fillet with vegetables) 102, *103*
mirin 106, 153, 218
modum-hwe (assorted raw and pickled fish) 150–53, *151*, *152*
modum-pyeonyuk (assorted boiled cuts of meat) 210, *211*
moyakgwa (square flaky pastry with honey) 233
mugeunji (aged *kimchi*) 150, 153
  dressing 153
mushrooms 218
  euni 40, 194
  golden enoki (*hwanggeum paengi-beoseot*) 136
  lion's mane (*norugungdengi-beoseot*) 136
  meok 134
  oyster (*neutari-beoseot*) 130, 136, 196
  pine 48, 102, 128, 136
  rock ear (*seogi-beoseot*) 94, 164, 167, 210, 214–17
  seogi 40, 128, 164, 187, 202
  shiitake 38, 44, 50, 52, 78, 80, 102, 104, 130, 136, 148, 160, 198, 210, 214
  shingled hedgehog (*neungi-beoseot*) 24, 136
mussels 62, 192, 232
  Korean 52
mustard, leaf 164, 167
mustard sauce 78, 94

N

naengmyeon (cold noodles) 92, *93*
neungi-songyi-beoseot-bap 136, *137*
Nohwa-do Island 76
nokdu-nongma-guksu (mung bean noodles with pine nut oil) 100, *101*
nuts
  chestnuts 62, 126, 134, 162, 164, 167, 202, 232
  Korean 50, 153, 208
  ginkgo 40, 164, 167, 214
  pine 22, 28, 30, 44, 47, 58, 96, 108, 144, 162, 164, 167, 190, 204, 208, 220
  walnuts 40, 108

O

octopus 40, 150, 164, 167, 208, 214–17, 232
  giant Pacific 153
ogokbap and ahop namul (five-grain rice and eight vegetables) 32–35, *33*, *34*

oi-seon (chilled cucumber with beef broth) 96, *97*, 233
okjamhwa-kkot-ssam (marinated beef wrapped with August-lilies) 148, *149*
oligosaccharide syrup 44, 47, 60, 108, 132, 142, 153
onban (hot soup with rice) 196, *197*
onion juice 104
oysters 164, 232
    beotgul 187

P

parae, dried (green laver seaweed) 76
pears 92
    Korean 26, 28, 76, 78, 80, 86, 134, 148, 164, 187, 208, 220, 232
    juice 190, 218
pepper, Sichuan 132
peppers
    chilli 56, 62, 64, 108, 154, 160
    green 132, 194
    red 84, 88, 132, 187, 194, 198, 232
    shishito 56
perilla leaves 132, 160
perilla oil 32, 35, 58, 82, 108, 136, 184, 192, 194, 200
plum extract 132
    Korean 153, 206
pomegranate seeds 208
pork 52, 64, 84, 86, 106, 160, 210, 218
potatoes 56, 182
prawns (shrimp) 26, 40, 50, 56, 62, 76, 140, 150, 156
    northern 153
    sauce 156
pufferfish 196, 206
    river (*hwang-bok*) 48, *72–73*
    skin jelly 206
pyeonyuk 210

R

radishes 102
    Korean 50, 62, 153, 164, 167, 214, 218
    white 24, 32, 35, 40, 78, 92, 132, 192
    young 154
red snapper 38
rice 58, 60, 88, 126, 136, 182, 220
    brown rice vinegar 76
    glutinous 104, 146, 162
    flour 158
    short-grain 204
    starch 164, 167
    sticky 104, 160

rice flour 210
    glutinous 64, 233
rice porridge 126
rice vinegar 187
rice wine 26, 40, 76, 128, 170, 173, 184, 218

S

saeujeot (fermented prawn/shrimp) 164, 167
sake 153
Samhaeju 239
sangchu (Korean lettuce) 132
saseul-jeok (beef and fish skewers) 82, *83*
seokryu-mandu (pomegranate dumpling) 24, *25*
seolya-myeok-jeok (grilled and lightly marinated beef) 190, *191*
seonji (blood clot) 160
sesame, ground 198
sesame seeds 142, 153, 186, 190, 222
sikhye (sweet rice drink) 220
sogogi and *dwaejigogi jangttaengi* (beef and pork pancake) 64
sogogi jangttaengi (beef pancake) 64
soju (Korean hard liquor) 60
sok-mieum (dates and ginseng porridge) 146, *147*
Songdo-sikhye (sweet rice drink with fruits) 220, *221*
songyi-jeon-bok-tang (pine mushrooms and abalone soup) 128, *129*
soondae (Korean sausage) 80
    Gaeseong-style (*jeolchang*) 160
    grilled 160, *161*
sorghum flour 64
soybeans 58
spinach 78
starch powder (*nongma*) 48, 52, 54, 96, 100, 102, 104, 108, 156, 158
sugar syrup 202
sujebi (hand-pulled buckwheat noodles) 154
sujeung-gye (chicken stuffed with mushroom filling) 104, *105*
sweet potato starch noodles 194

T

tangpyeong-chae (mung bean jelly salad with vegetables and beef) 44–47, *45*, *46*
taros 182
tea 247, *248*
tea leaves, green 153
thistle stalks 58

tofu 24, 48, 50, 52, 58, 80, 94, 156, 160, 186, 198, 214–17
tomatoes 76
tteok strips 94
tteok-mandu-guk (rice cake soup with dumplings) 198, *199*

U

ueong-japchae (stir-fried *ueong* and sweet potato noodles) 194, *195*

V

vegetables 32–35
vinegar water, sweet 187

W

wanja (Korean meatballs) 214–17
watermelons 94
wine, cooking 28, 187
wumpa bulgogi (*bulgogi* with spring onion/scallion) 30, *31*

Y

yak-bap (sweet glutinous rice with nuts and jujube) 162, *163*
yakgwa 170
yang (large cow intestines) 90
yeolguja-tang-ban (royal hot pot with rice) 214–17, *215*, *216*
yeongeun-jeon (lotus root pancake) 140, *141*
yeongye-gilgyeong-on-ban (rice with chicken and *doraji*) 182, *183*
yeonjeoyuk-jjim (braised pork) 86, *87*
yeorum pyeonyuk (slices of boiled meat) 84, *85*
yuja (*yuzu*) 202, 220
    citron marmalade 42
yuja-jumeoni (*yuja* citron pouch) 202, *203*
yuk-myeon jeontguk-gui (grilled beef noodle seasoned with pickled prawn/shrimp sauce) 28, *29*
yukgaejang (spicy beef and vegetable soup) 90
yukpo-dasik (pressed cookie made of beef jerky) 144, *145*
yumil-gwa (confectionery) 170, 222, 233

On the front cover:
Jindalae hwajeon (Azalea rice cake). Photo by Hee kee Min.

On the back cover:
Above left: Goryeo Celadon. Photo by Koo Bohnchang; below left: *Daeha jeonbok yukjeup muchim* (prawn and abalone with beef gravy). Photo by Hee kee Min; right: Onjium's fruit and vegetable marmalades. Photo by Hee kee Min.

First published in South Korea in 2016 under the title *Selected Recipes* and in 2022 under the title *Roots and Wings* by Onjium, Research Institute for Korean Cultural Heritage under Joongang Hwadong Foundation.

First published in the United Kingdom in 2026 by
Thames & Hudson Ltd, 6–24 Britannia Street, London WC1X 9JD

First published in the United States of America in 2026 by
Thames & Hudson Inc., 500 Fifth Avenue, New York, New York 10110

The Art of Korean Cooking © 2026 Thames & Hudson Ltd, London

Text and photographs © 2026 Onjium, Research Institute for Korean Cultural Heritage under Joongang Hwadong Foudation, unless otherwise stated.

Foreword © 2026 Woongchul Park

For additional picture credits, see page 251

Designed by Tim George

All Rights Reserved. No part of this publication may be reproduced or transmitted in any form or by any means, electronic or mechanical, including photocopy, recording or any other information storage and retrieval system, without prior permission in writing from the publisher.

EU Authorized Representative: Interart S.A.R.L.
19 rue Charles Auray, 93500 Pantin, Paris, France
productsafety@thameshudson.co.uk
interart.fr

A CIP catalogue record for this book is available from the British Library
Library of Congress Control Number 2025940871
ISBN 978-0-500-02954-1

01

Printed and bound in China by C&C Offset Printing Co., Ltd.

Be the first to know about our new releases, exclusive content and author events by visiting
thamesandhudson.com
thamesandhudsonusa.com
thamesandhudson.com.au

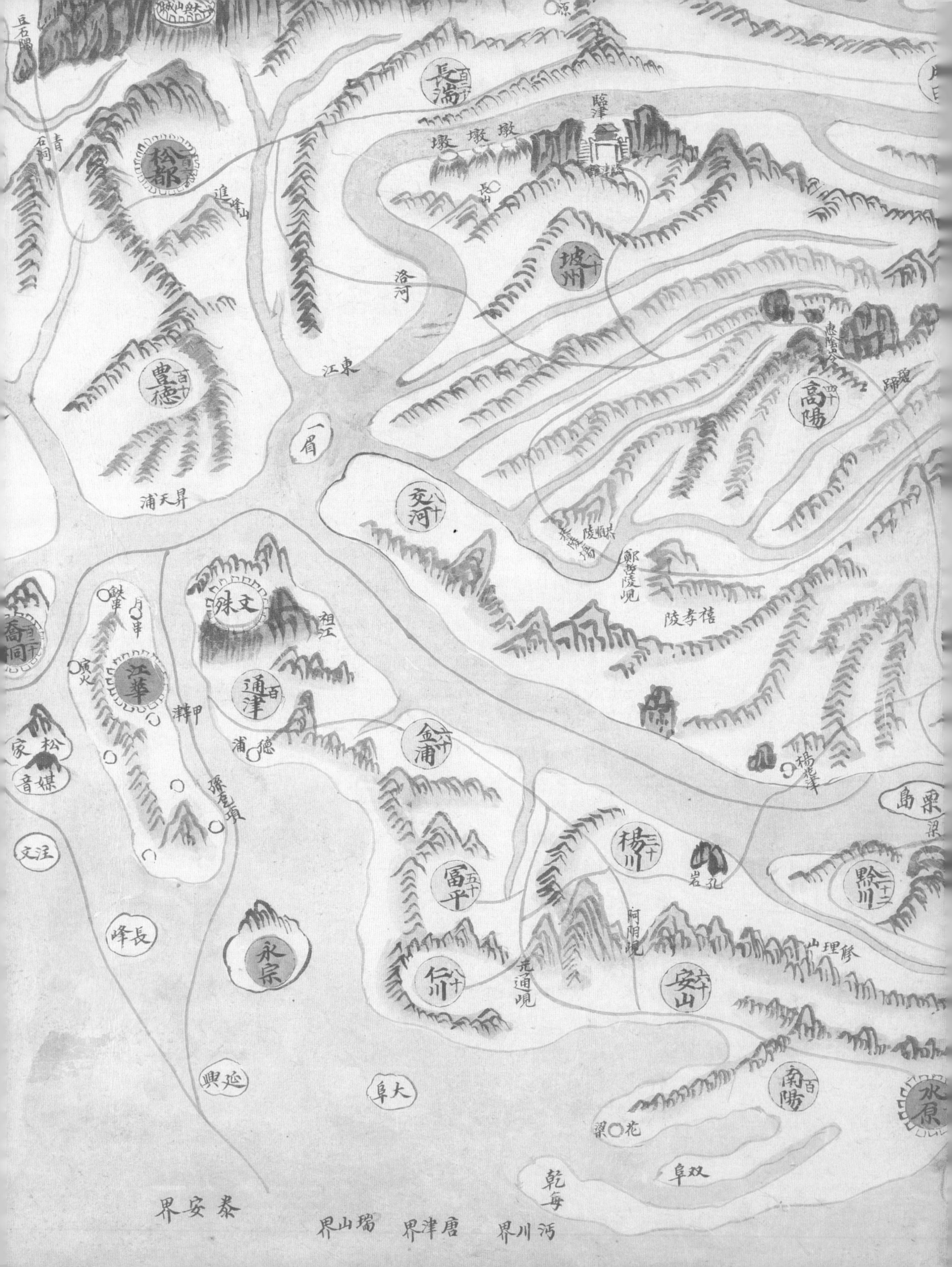